# Lunchbox food

# Lunchbox food

## Deona Tait

**HUMAN & ROUSSEAU**

**CAPE TOWN • PRETORIA • JOHANNESBURG**

Dedicated to Gary and Melissa

Cover photograph: Curried pasta and chicken salad with
mango and fruit salad (p. 69)

Copyright © 1998 by Deona Tait
First published in 1998 by Human & Rousseau (Pty) Ltd
State House, 3-9 Rose Street, Cape Town
Photography by Willie van Heerden
English translation by Annelene van der Merwe
Dishes prepared by Myrna Klerck
Styling by Myrna Klerck
Accessories supplied by Myrna Klerck
Typography and cover design by Chérie Collins
Text electronically pepared and set in 11 on 13 pt Garamond
by Human & Rousseau
Colour reproduction by Unifoto, Cape Town
Printed and bound by Colorcraft, Hong Kong

ISBN 0 7981 3841 6

# Contents

# Introduction

Most of us are compelled by our modern, fast-paced lifestyles to have at least one of our daily meals away from home. Takeaway meals should, therefore, meet at least one-third of our daily nutritional requirements.

The contents of lunch boxes are important to school-going children and working adults alike; correct nutrition, or the lack thereof, affects not only our productivity and performance, but also our stamina. Furthermore, a takeaway lunch frequently constitutes the only meal people have between a rushed early-morning breakfast and a quick late-afternoon snack when they get home.

It stands to reason, therefore, that takeaway food requires thorough planning. It should be well balanced, manageable, easy to eat and interesting into the bargain. Make it as tempting as possible so the packed lunch will become something to look forward to each day. The more attractive and inviting the contents of the lunch box, the smaller the temptation to buy sweets or junk food!

The recipes in this book are mainly aimed at meals that can be taken to school or work, but there are also a great many snacks that are perfect for picnics, for staving off hunger pangs while on holiday or for taking along on a journey.

Paging through the book, you will find something to suit every taste and occasion, and more than enough recipes and ideas to ensure that takeaway foods will never again be drab and boring!

*Clockwise from left back: stuffed bread (p. 39), poppy seed muffins (p. 55), lemon muffin (p. 57), Trix's quick gazpacho (p. 29), home-made pita breads (p. 49), quick buttermilk rusks (p. 113) and Diana's high-fibre rusks (p. 113)*

## What should a takeaway meal consist of?

Like any other balanced meal it should include starch, protein and fruit or vegetables. Picnic food or a meal taken on a long journey should meet the same requirements.

* A **starchy food**, such as bread, usually constitutes the most important part of a takeaway meal. Naturally, whole-wheat or brown bread should be your first choice as it is more nutritious and will keep your appetite satisfied for longer. All kinds of bread, rolls, pitas, muffins, scones, green mealies (quartered or halved), vetkoek, potato salad or baked potatoes may serve as starchy foods.

* A **high-protein** food such as meat, fish, egg or nuts, or a dairy product such as cheese, milk or yoghurt, must be included. A little fish paste or meat extract on a sandwich is not enough; at least 25 ml is required for it to count as a high-protein filling.

* A **fruit** or **vegetable** can be included in various guises: carrot strips, radishes, celery stalks, a tomato, a salad (fruit or vegetable), a fresh fruit, a fruit or vegetable kebab and a vegetable pie or tart. By way of a change, stewed fruit may be included.

* **Beverages** such as milk, milk drinks, rooibos tea drinks, vegetable drinks, fruit drinks or pure fruit juice are refreshing in summer, while soup kept warm in a wide-necked vacuum flask will banish the winter cold.

* **Sweet treats** such as biscuits, rusks with tea or coffee, dried fruit, fruit sweets or cake may also be included, but are not essential.

# Hints for preparing take-away meals

* Maintain a high standard of **hygiene** when preparing takeaway meals.
* It is advisable to prepare takeaway food **the night before** and refrigerate it overnight. As mornings are usually chaotic, it's easy to compromise and fill the lunch box with junk food instead of a nutritious meal.
* Make the necessary **preparations**, for example hard-boiling eggs (they can be refrigerated for up to a week), rinsing, drying and refrigerating lettuce in airtight plastic containers, slicing cooked meat, frying bacon until crisp, grating cheese and chopping nuts. Once all the ingredients have been prepared your child can easily help you assemble the meal. Do encourage your children to help – in this way they can also make sure that their favourite foods are included.
* Prepare a variety of **sandwich fillings** and store them in the refrigerator.
* Small containers of fruit and vegetable juice may be packed in their **frozen** state. By the time they're needed they will have thawed but still be refreshingly cold. See to it that the containers are leakproof.
* Guard against drying out by packaging food in **airtight materials** such as aluminium foil, plastic and plastic containers.
* Wrap different foods **separately** to prevent blending of flavours and foods.
* Food (for a picnic, for example) can be kept **warm** for a short while by wrapping it well in aluminium foil, with the shiny side facing in. Insulate the parcel by wrapping it in several layers of newsprint.
* Keep **cold** food (for a picnic, for example) **cold** by chilling it well in the refrigerator beforehand and then placing it in a cool bag or wrapping it in aluminium foil and several layers of newsprint.
* Keep takeaway food in the **coolest place possible** until needed.
* Make a separate heading for takeaway food on your **shopping list**, and vary the ingredients.
* **Variety** is of the utmost importance. Lunch boxes should not contain the same offerings day after day.

Sandwiches may even be cut into different shapes, or consist of different breads in combination, such as rye and white bread.

* The food should be **easily manageable** and one should be able to pick it up with the fingers, or eat it with a fork only.
* Use **interesting food containers** – they will make the meal all the more inviting. Ensure that the containers have tight-fitting lids to prevent drying out.
* Include a **surprise treat** occasionally, such as a whole-meal cookie, a dried-fruit roll, a piece of biltong or dried sausage or dried fruit on a skewer.
* A takeaway meal should be neither too sophisticated **nor too ordinary**.
* Try to present food as **attractively** as possible; use **garnishes** such as a sprig of parsley, or a carrot or sweet pepper cut into julienne strips.
* Provide **plastic cutlery** with, for example, a salad or food that has to be reheated.
* Use **plastic** or **paper plates** and remember to include salt, pepper and paper serviettes, where necessary.
* Be on the lookout for **small containers** for salt and pepper or favourite **flavourings** that will fit into the lunch box.
* Reserve **a few carrots,** celery stalks and a piece of cucumber for takeaway meals while preparing them for home use.
* If **fruit** has to stay in the lunch box for longer than half a day, it's better to keep it whole than to cut it up for a fruit salad.
* A **hard-boiled** egg will keep longer in its shell.
* Slice meat **very thinly** or flake it for sandwich fillings – it will be much easier to eat. It is also easier to eat thin, stacked slices than a single thick slice.
* If cold meat is to be used in a salad, cut it into strips and **marinate** overnight in a flavoursome sauce.
* All **salad ingredients** should be as **fresh** as possible. Prepare salad dressings beforehand and store them in separate containers, since green salad ingredients will wilt if salad dressing is added in advance.
* A **fresh fruit** makes an excellent **dessert** for any takeaway meal.

# Freezing

If your weeks are very busy, prepare and freeze take-away food during the weekends to save time.

## SANDWICHES

Sandwiches in airtight packaging may be frozen. Depending on the fillings, they will keep for up to 3 weeks. Prepare a week's supply of sandwiches and freeze them in individual plastic or aluminium foil parcels. Thaw them in their packaging material, or put them in the lunch box in their frozen state; by the time they're eaten the bread will have thawed.

The following fillings can be frozen: combinations of boiled, mashed egg yolk (not the egg white), biltong, peanut butter, drained, grated pineapple, any kind of cold meat, sour cream, cream cheese, apple sauce, pickles and chopped bacon.

Avoid freezing mayonnaise and salad dressings which contain vinegar and may separate during the freezing process. Ingredients with a high water content, especially tomatoes, cucumber and lettuce, will make the sandwiches soggy.

Remember that some seasonings will change during freezing: pepper becomes stronger, herbs develop a sharper flavour and salt loses some of its taste.

## MUFFINS

A variety of muffins may be baked, frozen and taken along in their frozen state; by playtime or teatime they will have thawed. Muffins should be frozen in airtight packaging as soon as possible: first place them, uncovered, on a cooling rack in the freezer for 15-30 minutes, then transfer them to an airtight plastic bag or container, or simply wrap them singly in clingwrap and freeze immediately. A single frozen muffin can easily be removed from the plastic bag or container and put in the lunch box. It will take an hour to thaw at room temperature.

If you don't like the idea of putting a frozen muffin in the lunch box, microwave it on a piece of paper towelling on 100% power for 30-40 seconds. Remember to pierce the clingwrap covering first.

## FLAVOURED AND OTHER INSTANT BREADS

Instant breads can successfully be frozen whole or sliced. Wrap the completely cooled loaf tightly in plastic or heavy aluminium foil and freeze for up to 3 months. Thaw at room temperature for 4-6 hours, or cover with damp paper towelling and microwave on 30% power for 4 minutes, depending on its size.

## PANCAKES

Cool the cooked pancakes completely. Separate them with sheets of waxed paper or Foilene and freeze in airtight packaging or containers for up to 3 months. Thaw the pancakes at room temperature, on 30% power in the microwave oven or over a saucepan of boiling water. The thawed pancakes may also be heated over boiling water.

Uncooked pancake batter may be frozen for a few weeks only. Pour the batter into a jug with a tight-fitting lid. It may be thawed in the same jug.

## PIES

Both cooked and uncooked pies may be frozen for up to 2 months. Cool cooked pies completely before freezing, and glaze uncooked pies, if preferred, to save time later. Pie fillings may also be prepared and frozen for later use.

First remove the packaging material, then reheat cooked pies in the oven at 180 ˚C for about 10 minutes, depending on size.

Uncooked frozen pies may be baked without thawing them first. Glaze the pies (if it was not done before freezing) and place on a greased baking tray. Bake at 200 ˚C for 10-12 minutes longer than the time required for reheating cooked pies. Cool and put in the lunch box.

Reheating a pie in the microwave oven will spoil its taste. If this is your only option, however, microwave it on 50-70% power for the best results. A microwave wrap for browning and crispening pastry is available from supermarkets. Wrap the pie in this material and microwave on 100% power: 3-3½ minutes for a thawed pie and 4-4½ minutes for a frozen one.

## SOUP

Soup which is properly covered may be refrigerated for 2-3 days. If poured into suitable individual containers and tightly sealed it may be frozen for 2-3 months. Remove the frozen soup from the freezer in good time and thaw overnight in the refrigerator, or put the frozen soup in the lunch box; it will have thawed by lunch time. If there are no reheating facilities at work, reheat the soup at home and pour it into a wide-necked flask.

## COOKED MEAT

If, for the sake of convenience, you wish to cook and freeze meat in advance for later use in takeaway meals, bear the following in mind:
* Maintain strict standards of hygiene while preparing meat.
* Use salt sparingly, as it hastens rancidity and loss of meat juices.
* An excessive quantity of garlic tends to develop an "off taste" during freezing.
* To prevent overcooking, it is advisable to cook meat destined for the freezer for a shorter time than the recommended cooking time. The cooking process will be completed during reheating.
* Cool the cooked dish completely before wrapping it for the freezer. Don't forget to label it.
* Avoid ingredients that don't freeze well:
- The texture of starchy foods, such as pasta, potatoes and rice, tends to change during the freezing process. These foods should be frozen only if they're part of a sauce; if not, add them during reheating.
- Use little or no cream in sauces: cream sauces tend to separate after freezing. If you do freeze a cream sauce, however, reheat it over boiling water in a double boiler while stirring continuously.
- Parsley, lettuce and celery become mushy.
- The flavours of spices such as curry and pepper become stronger during freezing.
- Excess fat.

If these guidelines are followed and the dish is frozen in airtight packaging, it will keep in the freezer for up to 2 months.

*Front: Vetkoek (p. 51), stuffed with savoury mince with tomato (p. 42) and kisses (p. 115). Centre: chicken curry triangles (p. 84) and pizza with salami (p. 89). Back: spicy chicken drumsticks (p. 106)*

# MENUS

The following menus will give you a good idea of what to put in the lunch box from Mondays to Fridays. There are also suggestions for an office party, a picnic and food for a long journey.

## MONDAY-TO-FRIDAY MENU
### (with reheating facilities)

### MONDAY

Flavoursome tomato soup (p. 23)
Whole-wheat rolls with avocado and lettuce
Date and raisin balls (p. 123)

### TUESDAY

Bacon and mushroom pasta dish (p. 102)
Vegetable kebabs (p. 80)
Slice of banana cake (p. 121)

### WEDNESDAY

Baked potato (p. 95) with spinach filling (p. 43)
Slice of ham or cold meat
Chocolate chip cookie (p. 119)

### THURSDAY

Sandwich with a slice of leftover chicken, cucumber
slices and sandwich spread
Fruit yoghurt

### FRIDAY

Picnic tartlets (p. 83)
Fresh fruit, e.g. pear
Chocolate marshmallow squares (p. 123)

Remember to include something to drink.

## MONDAY-TO-FRIDAY MENU
### (without reheating facilities)

### MONDAY

Hamburgers (p. 38) with whole-wheat buns, tomato,
lettuce and
gherkins or cucumber
Fresh fruit
Almond and caramel bars (p. 118)

### TUESDAY

Marinated mushrooms on skewers (p. 81) in a hot-dog
roll spread with garlic butter
Biltong sticks (p. 111)
Fruit yoghurt

### WEDNESDAY

Trix's quick gazpacho
(chilled tomato soup; p. 29)
Whole-wheat roll with flaked smoked snoek, gherkins
and cottage cheese
Fruit roll

### THURSDAY

Apple loaf (p. 46) with butter
Vienna and cheese kebabs (p. 77)
Debra's health triangles (oats cookies; p. 117)

### FRIDAY

Crudités (p. 72) with a dip (p. 17)
Whole-wheat yeast batter bread (p. 47)
Stuffed eggs (p. 19)
Flavoured popcorn (p. 20)

Remember to include something to drink.

# MENUS

## MENU FOR AN OFFICE PARTY

Dried-fruit compote (p. 15)
Bread wheels with tongue filling (p. 41)
Individual snoek quiches (p. 92)
Concertina steak strips (p. 75)
Crudités (p. 72)
Dips (p. 17)
Pâtés and spreads
with savoury biscuits
Rainbow kebabs (p. 80)
Miracle squares (chocolate and
mocha cake squares; p. 121)

## PICNIC MENU

Bobotie snacks (p. 105)
Spicy chicken drumsticks (p. 106)

Stuffed bread (p. 39)
Crudités (p. 72)
Fruit salad (p. 69)
Caramel and sultana balls (p. 124)

## PACK-AND-GO MENU

Home-made pita breads with salad filling
(salad dressing separate; p. 49)
Sandwiches with egg filling
(p. 33), avocado filling and
bully beef spread (p. 32)
Savoury meatballs (p. 106)
Vegetable tartlets (p. 83)
Fruit kebabs (p. 80)
or fresh fruit
Snack mixture
(p. 21)

# This and that

## Microwave muesli

Keep a jar of muesli and powdered milk at the office, or take along yoghurt to complement it, and you may not even have to eat breakfast before leaving home in the mornings.

    80 g oats (250 ml)
    50 ml digestive bran
    50 ml coconut
    50 ml wheat germ
    50 ml Nutty Wheat
    15 ml sesame seeds
    30 ml sunflower seeds
    30 ml flaked almonds
    pinch salt
    50 ml honey or brown sugar
    2,5 ml vanilla essence
    30 ml cooking oil
    30 ml boiling water

Combine oats, bran, coconut, wheat germ, Nutty Wheat, sesame seeds, sunflower seeds, almonds and salt. Mix honey or brown sugar, vanilla essence, oil and water. Using a fork or your fingertips, blend oil mixture and dry ingredients well. Turn mixture into a 220 mm microwave pie dish, spreading it evenly, and microwave for 5 minutes on full power. Stir well to remove all lumps. Microwave for a further minute on full power or until golden brown. Allow to cool and transfer to a glass jar with a lid.

Makes about 750 ml

---

VARIATION
* Chopped dried fruit, such as apple rings or raisins, and nuts may be added.

---

*Microwave muesli and dried-fruit compote*

## Dried-fruit compote

The longer this compote is stored in the refrigerator the tastier it will be, as the flavours need ample time to blend. It can be refrigerated in a sealed glass jar for up to 6 weeks. And don't worry about the effects of the alcohol – it all evaporates when the liquid is brought to the boil.

    a piece of orange or lemon peel
    2 cinnamon sticks
    2 whole cloves
    250 ml rooibos tea
    250 ml orange juice
    250 ml brandy or rum
    75 ml white sugar
    250 g prunes
    250 g dried apple rings
    250 g dried apricots

Tie citrus peel, cinnamon sticks and cloves in a muslin bag and place in a saucepan along with remaining ingredients, except dried fruit. Bring to the boil and simmer, stirring continuously, until sugar has dissolved. Remove muslin bag. Using a slotted spoon, layer dried fruit into sterilised glass jars and pour hot liquid over. Allow to cool, then seal.

Makes 8 servings

**TO TAKE ALONG:** Nuts (packed separately).

HINT
* To pack, use a slotted spoon to transfer dried fruit to a plastic container with a lid. Add a little sauce, if preferred.

# CHUTNEY, MUSTARD SAUCE AND FLAVOURED MAYONNAISE

Delicious chutney, mayonnaise and mustard sauce can completely transform sandwiches and other takeaway meals! Use chutney with cold bobotie or cold meat, for example, and mustard sauce with ham, corned meat, frankfurters or pork sausages. Spoon a little chutney or mustard sauce into a small jar and pack together with meatballs, pies or cold meats.

## Banana and raisin chutney

    400 g banana slices
    1 sweet pepper, seeded and chopped
    1 large onion, chopped
    1 clove garlic, crushed
    125 g raisins (210 ml)
    salt and freshly ground black pepper to taste
    5 ml mild curry powder
    3 ml turmeric
    375 ml vinegar
    200 g sugar (250 ml)

Mix all the ingredients in a saucepan. Slowly bring to the boil and simmer for 1 hour, stirring regularly, until chutney has reached the desired consistency. Spoon into a jar and refrigerate.

Makes 750 ml

## Tomato chutney

    500 g ripe tomatoes, skinned and coarsely chopped
    2 onions, chopped
    100 g brown sugar (125 ml)
    125 ml vinegar

    75 ml sultanas
    15 ml dry mustard
    5 ml ground ginger
    5 ml salt
    1 ml cayenne pepper

Mix all the ingredients in a saucepan. Slowly bring to the boil and simmer for 1 hour, stirring regularly, until chutney has reached the desired consistency. Spoon into a jar and refrigerate.

Makes about 750 ml

## Uncooked mustard sauce

This sauce can also be refrigerated for a long time. It is delicious served with any kind of cold meat and may even be used as a dip for meat snacks or cocktail sausages.

    150 ml mayonnaise
    100 g condensed milk (¼ of 397 g tin)
    100 ml mustard sauce

Mix all the ingredients and spoon into a screw-topped jar. Store in the refrigerator.

Makes about 375 ml

## Cooked mustard sauce with herbs

This sauce may also be used for potato salad or cooked onion salad.

    2 small eggs
    60 g sugar (75 ml)
    salt to taste
    10 ml dry mustard

125 ml white vinegar
5 ml dried mixed herbs or 10 ml each fresh or 5 ml each
    dried chives, origanum and dill
5 ml crushed mustard seeds
125 ml sour cream

Beat eggs well. Gradually add sugar, salt and mustard, beating well. Gradually add vinegar. Stir mixture over boiling water until thickened. Allow to cool, then add herbs, mustard seeds and sour cream. Store in an airtight jar in the refrigerator.

Makes about 300 ml

# Flavoured mayonnaise

A flavoured mayonnaise will pep up sandwiches, stuffed eggs and even cold meats. Store in a jar in the refrigerator.

* **Tomato mayonnaise:** Add 20 ml tomato paste, ½ small onion, chopped, a pinch of sugar and 30 ml chopped fresh parsley to 250 ml mayonnaise. Mix thoroughly.
* **Tartar sauce:** Add 1 chopped gherkin, 15 ml chopped chives, 15 ml chopped fresh parsley, 5 ml prepared mustard, 5 ml lemon juice, 25 ml sandwich spread and 5 ml sugar to 250 ml mayonnaise. Mix thoroughly.
* **Herbed mayonnaise:** Add 30 ml chopped fresh parsley and 15 ml chopped chives to 250 ml mayonnaise. Mix thoroughly. (Note: Dried herbs will impart a different taste.)
* **Spinach mayonnaise:** Add 150 ml blanched spinach, drained and coarsely chopped, 30 ml each chopped fresh parsley and chives and 30 ml coarsely chopped mixed pickles to 250 ml mayonnaise. Mix thoroughly.
* **Green-peppercorn mayonnaise:** Add 25 ml crushed Madagascar green peppercorns to 250 ml mayonnaise.

# DIPS

Prepare dips for hard-boiled egg wedges, savoury biscuits, Melba toast, tortilla slices, small meatballs on cocktail sticks, Vienna sausages and cheese cubes on cocktail sticks, as well as crudités. Pour the dips into small wide-necked jars with lids, ready for use.

# Onion dip

1 packet white onion soup powder
500 ml milk
1 x 250 g tub smooth cottage cheese

Mix soup powder and milk in a saucepan. Slowly bring to the boil and simmer for a few minutes. Allow to cool, then stir in cottage cheese. Spoon into dip bowls with lids and refrigerate until needed.

Makes about 650 ml

# Curry-flavoured dip

1 x 250 g tub smooth cottage cheese
10 ml curry powder
30-50 ml cream
15 ml lemon juice
10 ml tomato sauce
30 ml chutney

Mix ingredients, spoon into dip bowls with lids and refrigerate until needed.

Makes about 350 ml

# Tomato dip

1 x 43 g packet savoury white sauce or 250 ml thick
    white sauce
250 ml mayonnaise
250 ml tomato sauce

Prepare white sauce according to instructions on packet
and allow to cool. (Use only 200 ml milk instead of 250 ml
as indicated.) Mix sauce, mayonnaise and tomato sauce.
Spoon into dip bowls with lids. Refrigerate until needed.

Makes about 750 ml

# Seafood dip

1 x 43 g packet savoury white sauce
25 ml mayonnaise
5 ml lemon juice
1 clove garlic, crushed
1 x 105 g tin smoked oysters or mussels, coarsely
    chopped
paprika

Prepare white sauce according to instructions on packet.
Allow to cool. Add the rest of the ingredients, except paprika, to white sauce and mix well. Spoon into dip bowls
with lids and sprinkle with paprika. Refrigerate until needed.

Makes about 350 ml

# Avocado dip

1 ripe avocado
30 ml lemon juice
1 small onion, finely chopped, or 4-6 chives, chopped
1 clove garlic, crushed
salt, freshly ground black pepper and paprika to taste
sprig of fresh parsley (optional)
125 ml plain yoghurt, cream cheese or thick cream

Peel avocado, remove pip and cube flesh. Sprinkle with
lemon juice. Place all the ingredients in a food processor and process until smooth. Spoon into dip bowls
with lids and refrigerate until needed.

Makes about 350 ml

# FLAVOURED BUTTERS

Flavoured butters are not used for steaks only, but also in
baked potatoes (p. 95), to impart a special flavour to sandwiches, and even for incorporating with pasta. Keep a few
flavoured butters in the refrigerator or freezer to add interest to ordinary sandwich fillings.

---

### How to make a flavoured butter

Cream butter, add desired flavourings and mix thoroughly.
Place butter on a piece of aluminium foil, clingwrap or waxed
paper and press into a sausage shape, using aluminium foil.
Wrap and roll lightly. Refrigerate until firm, or freeze.

---

VARIATIONS
* **Butter with mixed herbs:** Mix 125 g butter, 2 chopped
  chives or 10 ml chopped onion, 50 ml chopped fresh
  mixed herbs (thyme, marjoram, origanum and rosemary)
  or 20 ml dried mixed herbs, and 10 ml lemon juice. It is
  delicious in baked potatoes or sandwiches made with
  cold chicken, beef or lamb.
* **Lemon butter:** Mix 125 g butter, 10 ml lemon juice and
  2 cloves garlic, crushed. Use in sandwiches made with
  avocado or other salad ingredients.
* **Mustard butter:** Mix 125 g butter and 10 ml prepared
  mustard or 5 ml dry mustard. Spread on a hot dog or
  hamburger, or serve with beef, lamb or pork.
* **Caper butter:** Mix 100 g butter, 10 ml chopped capers,
  5 ml lemon juice, 5 ml grated lemon rind, 1 crushed clove
  garlic and 2 ml prepared mustard. Ideal for baked potatoes or beef and lamb.

# STUFFED EGGS

Stuffed eggs can be prepared a day in advance and refrigerated before packing them the next morning. When spooning the stuffing into the egg white halves, level it to ensure that the halves will fit together perfectly. Wrap the eggs in aluminium foil or clingwrap to keep the two halves together. Alternatively, the eggs may be wrapped in lettuce leaves before adding the aluminium foil or clingwrap.

> VARIATIONS
> * Mix with egg yolks and use as a filling:
> - 100 ml grated cheese, 5 ml French mustard and 20 ml yoghurt or mayonnaise;
> - 100 ml finely chopped ham and 25 ml mayonnaise;
> - 100 ml grated cheese, 25 ml chutney and 3 ml curry powder;
> - chopped, crisply fried bacon;
> - mustard, tomato sauce and curry powder or chutney.

## Basic recipe

6 hard-boiled eggs
15 ml mayonnaise or yoghurt, or 25 ml smooth cottage cheese or smooth cottage cheese with chives
salt and pepper

Shell and halve eggs. Remove yolks, then mash and moisten them with mayonnaise, yoghurt or cottage cheese. Season with salt and pepper. Spoon mixture into egg white halves and fit the halves together again.

### How to hard-boil eggs

* Add 15 ml vinegar to the water to prevent water marks in the saucepan.
* Prick the rounded ends of the eggs and place them in tap water in a saucepan to prevent the shells from cracking.
* Calculate the cooking time from the moment the water starts to boil.
* Cooking times: hard – 10 minutes; medium – 6-7 minutes; and soft – 3-4 minutes.
* Crack the eggs immediately after the cooking process and immerse them in cold water. This makes them easier to shell and prevents blue rings forming around the yolks.

# COOL DRINKS

## Fruit drink

A refreshing fruit beverage for small cool-drink bottles! Double the recipe if you wish to use the full quantity of fruit squash and a sufficiently large container is available. The fruit drink will keep well outside the refrigerator.

6 bananas
1 papino, peeled and coarsely chopped, or ½ pawpaw, peeled and coarsely chopped
½ pineapple, peeled and coarsely chopped
300 g sugar (375 ml)
½ x 60 g packet tartaric acid
3 litres water
1 x 110 g tin granadilla pulp
½ x 750 ml bottle each lemon and orange squash
500 ml apricot juice

Place fruit in a food processor or liquidiser and process until smooth. Dissolve sugar and tartaric acid in water in a 5-litre container. Add fruit purée and sugar solution to remaining ingredients. Mix well, then refrigerate.

Makes 5 litres

# Mixed fruit juice with mint

Mint tea is very refreshing, so it stands to reason that a mint extract will impart a distinctive flavour to a mixture of fruit juices.

Pack small containers of frozen fruit juice. When you get around to drinking it, it will have thawed but still be deliciously cold.

50 ml boiling water
5 ml dried or 15 ml chopped fresh mint
375 ml apple juice
125 ml orange and mango juice
125 ml pineapple juice

Pour boiling water over mint and allow to steep for 20-30 minutes. Meanwhile, mix fruit juices in a large jug. Strain mint extract and add to juice mixture. Refrigerate until needed.

± Makes 650 ml

# Mixed fruit juice with pineapple pieces

Prepare the juice and store it in a jug in the refrigerator. After giving the fruit juice a quick stir the children can fill their containers themselves.

1 litre orange juice
1 litre guava juice
1 x 440 g tin crushed pineapple, undrained

Mix orange and guava juices in a jug large enough for 3 litres juice. Add undrained pineapple and mix well. Refrigerate until needed.

Makes about 2,5 litres

# SNACKS

## Flavoured popcorn

Children love this sharp-flavoured popcorn and will also have lots of fun making it. When cooled, transfer to plastic bags.

50 ml cooking oil
8-litre saucepan with a lid
250 ml popcorn kernels

FLAVOURING MIXTURE
1 ml ground cumin
50 ml dried origanum
15 ml cayenne pepper (optional)

Pour oil into the large saucepan. Add popcorn kernels and heat over moderate heat. Cover with lid as soon as first kernels start popping. Carefully shake the saucepan from time to time, until all the kernels have stopped popping. Transfer popcorn to a bowl. Mix cumin, origanum and cayenne pepper, if used, and sprinkle over popcorn.

---

VARIATIONS
* **Popcorn with peanuts:** Melt 60 ml butter and add 5 ml seasoning salt and 125 ml peanuts. Add to popcorn in a dish with a lid, cover and shake well.
* **Popcorn with barbecue spice:** Melt 60 ml butter and stir in 20 ml barbecue spice and 5 ml paprika. Add to popcorn in a dish with a lid, cover and shake well.
* **Popcorn with herbs:** Melt 60 ml butter and stir in 5 ml instant chicken stock powder, 25 ml dried mixed herbs and a little onion salt. Add to popcorn in a dish with a lid, cover and shake well.

HINTS
* Make popcorn on a cool, dry day. If the air is too humid the popcorn will be tough.
* Use the size saucepan specified in the recipe. If you heat a too-large quantity of popcorn kernels in a too-small saucepan the lid might "pop" off, the popcorn at the bottom will burn and the popcorn will not puff up sufficiently.
* If you heat 75 ml popcorn kernels in a 3-litre saucepan you will get about 8 x 250 ml popcorn. If you have an 8-litre saucepan with a lid you can heat 250 ml kernels, making about 18 x 250 ml popcorn.
* Place popcorn kernels and oil in a cooking bag, then microwave.

# Snack mixture

Pack this nutritious snack mixture into plastic bags covered with brown-paper bags. The dried fruit may be varied according to taste.

100 g coarse coconut or oats (300 ml)
125 g dates, diced
150 g large raisins (250 ml)
150 g pitted prunes (250 ml)
150 g dried banana slices (250 ml)
1 x 250 g packet dried pears, cut into strips
1-2 x 100 g packets mixed nuts (250-500 ml)

Sprinkle coconut or oats over dates and mix carefully, but thoroughly, until coconut slightly adheres to the dates. Blend remaining ingredients well and add to dates.

VARIATIONS
* Spoil your family – and yourself – by adding 150 g, or less, chocolate pieces to the mixture, and have fun digging out the "treasures".
* Add 250 ml toasted sunflower seeds or unsalted peanuts.
* Toasting the coconut will add a special flavour.

HINT
* If you're going on a long journey, write each one's name on the paper bags containing the snacks.

# A flask of soup . . . ◆ ◆ ◆

## Flavoursome tomato soup

If you have neither the time nor the patience to make soup from scratch, experiment with packets and tins as demonstrated in this recipe.

1 medium onion, finely chopped
2 cloves garlic, crushed
10 ml cooking oil
1 x 61 g packet tomato soup powder
500 ml milk
350 ml boiling water
1 x 115 g tin shredded tuna in brine, undrained
15 ml dried or 50 ml chopped fresh parsley
freshly ground black pepper to taste

Fry onion and garlic in heated oil until onion is translucent. Add soup powder and stir-fry for 1 minute. Add milk and boiling water to onion mixture and slowly bring to the boil, stirring continuously. Simmer for 5 minutes, remove from heat and stir in tuna and parsley. Return to the stove and heat through. Season to taste.

Makes 4-6 servings

**TO TAKE ALONG:** Cheese muffins (p. 61).

HINT
* Combine, for example, two kinds of soup powders, such as cream of chicken and chicken noodle, and add a little leftover chicken – it will taste like the real thing. Oxtail soup and beef broth powders also combine extremely well.

*Spinach soup (p. 24) and three-bean soup (p. 25)*

## Pumpkin soup

1 large onion, chopped
piece of fresh ginger root, chopped
3 cloves garlic, crushed
50 ml butter
750 g uncooked pumpkin, peeled and cubed
500 ml water
500 ml chicken stock
1 cinnamon stick
juice and rind of 1 lemon
125 ml thick cream
salt and freshly ground black pepper to taste

Fry onion, ginger root and garlic in heated butter in a large, heavy-based saucepan. Add remaining ingredients, except cream and seasonings, and simmer for 15-20 minutes or until pumpkin is tender. Cool slightly, then remove cinnamon stick and purée soup. Add cream, season with salt and pepper and heat through.

Makes 4 servings

**TO TAKE ALONG:** Ham and cheese roll.

---

### Soup is the ideal takeaway food!

Heart-warming soup is one of the most economical meals you can have when you're strapped for cash – and it's nutritious and flavoursome into the bargain. Invest in a wide-necked vacuum flask specially for taking soup to work, and never leave home without it in winter! Soup can be refrigerated in a covered container for 2-3 days, or poured into suitable individual bowls, sealed and frozen for 2-3 months.

# Spinach soup

This quick and scrumptious soup can even be made in the morning before leaving for work – a real godsend to late risers.

    1 packet cream of chicken soup powder
    500 ml milk
    500 ml chicken stock
    1 x 250 g packet frozen creamed spinach, thawed
    grated nutmeg to taste
    salt and freshly ground black pepper to taste
    juice and grated rind of ½ lemon

Prepare cream of chicken soup with milk and stock according to instructions on packet. Add creamed spinach and heat through. Season soup with nutmeg, salt, pepper and lemon juice and rind.

Makes 3-4 servings

**TO TAKE ALONG:** Whole-wheat sandwich with avocado and bacon spread (p. 35).

---

VARIATION
* Replace a little of the chicken stock with white wine. Remember, the alcohol evaporates when heated, leaving only the delicious flavour.

---

HINT
* The creamed spinach is available in 2 x 250 g plastic bags in a box. Some kinds of creamed spinach contain feta cheese, among other things, which imparts a delicious flavour to the soup.

# Curried onion soup

    5 onions, sliced
    60 g butter
    15 ml mild curry powder
    60 ml cake flour
    1,5 litres chicken stock
    150 ml sour cream
    salt and freshly ground black pepper to taste
    chopped fresh parsley for garnishing

Fry onions in heated butter until translucent. Add curry powder and flour and stir-fry for 1-2 minutes. Stir in hot stock and simmer for 10 minutes. Cool slightly, then add sour cream. Process mixture in a food processor until smooth. Season soup with salt and pepper and heat through, but do not allow to boil. Pour into wide-necked vacuum flasks and sprinkle with parsley.

Makes 4 servings

**TO TAKE ALONG:** Whole-wheat sandwich with snoek filling (p. 43).

HINT
* Dissolve 2-3 chicken stock cubes in 1,5 litres boiling water if home-made chicken stock is unavailable.

---

### How to peel onions without tears

Blanch the onions in boiling water – the skins will also come off more easily. Alternatively, place the onions in the freezer for a few minutes before peeling them.

# Cheese soup

This soup can be prepared in a jiffy if you have all the required ingredients in your grocery cupboard.

125 g rindless bacon, chopped
1 large onion, chopped
1 leek, cut into rings
1 clove garlic, crushed
1 packet mushroom soup powder
1 litre water or chicken stock
250 g Cheddar cheese spread
salt and freshly ground black pepper to taste
250 ml cream
15 ml dried or 50 ml chopped fresh parsley

Fry bacon, onion, leek and garlic in a heavy-based saucepan until bacon is crisp. Add soup powder and stir-fry for 1 minute. Add hot water or stock and slowly bring to the boil. Simmer for 5 minutes. Stir in cheese spread and season with salt and pepper. Add cream and parsley and heat through.

Makes 3-4 servings

**TO TAKE ALONG:** Melba toast.

---

### How to make your own Melba toast

Halve a loaf of bread at least one or two days old. Remove the crusts and cut each half diagonally into two quarters to make a total of 4 bread triangles. Slice the triangles very thinly. Arrange the slices on a baking tray and bake in a preheated oven at 180 °C. Turn the slices frequently until the ends curl up and turn light brown.

HINTS
* One loaf of bread yields about 46 slices of Melba toast.
* Pack Melba toast together with a pâté or dip.
* Store Melba toast in an airtight container. It will keep for up to a month.
* Spread Melba toast with a flavoured butter, if preferred.

---

# Three-bean soup

Another quick soup that doesn't need hours to develop its flavour!

250 g rindless bacon, coarsely chopped
2 onions, chopped
2 cloves garlic, crushed
4 tomatoes, skinned and coarsely chopped
500 ml chicken stock
10-12 carrot tips or 2-3 medium carrots, sliced
3 ml each dried or 10 ml each chopped fresh basil and parsley
1 x 410 g tin beans in tomato sauce
1 x 410 g tin sliced green beans, undrained
1 x 410 g tin butter beans
salt and pepper to taste

Fry bacon until crisp, remove and set aside. Fry onions and garlic in bacon fat. Add tomatoes and braise for a few minutes. Add bacon along with stock, carrots and herbs. Simmer for 15 minutes or until carrots are tender. Add beans and heat through. Season with salt and pepper.

Makes 4-6 servings

**TO TAKE ALONG:** A small container of fried or toasted croutons; these can be frozen and used directly from the freezer.

HINTS
* Sauté one or two grated baby marrows with the onions and garlic.
* If the soup is to be a takeaway meal, it's advisable to grate the carrots and spoon the soup into a wide-necked vacuum flask.

# Shrimp and pea soup

A truly sumptuous soup!

   1 x 410 g tin tomato soup
   1 x 410 g tin pea soup
   375 ml milk
   1 x 190 g tin shrimps, drained
   25 ml medium sherry
   5 ml dried or 15 ml chopped fresh parsley (optional)
   125 ml cream
   Tabasco sauce, salt and black pepper to taste

Bring tomato soup, pea soup and milk just to the boil and simmer for 10 minutes. Add shrimps, sherry and parsley and heat through. Stir in cream and heat through, but do not allow to boil. Season with Tabasco sauce, salt and black pepper to taste.

Makes 4 servings

# Bean soup

This soup will be even tastier if reheated the next day. If you have neglected to soak the beans overnight, there is a quick method (see hint).

   500 g sugar beans (700 ml)
   1,5 kg sliced beef shin or mutton shank, 15 mm thick
   15 ml cooking oil
   4 onions, chopped
   2 cloves garlic, crushed
   2 carrots, sliced
   5 ml dried or 15 ml chopped fresh thyme
   2 sprigs parsley
   15 ml vinegar
   2 litres water or meat stock
   salt and freshly ground black pepper to taste
   3 bay leaves
   3 frankfurters, sliced (optional)

*Trix's quick gazpacho (p. 29)*

Soak beans overnight. Drain. Brown meat in heated cooking oil. Add onions and garlic and fry until onions are translucent. Add beans and remaining ingredients, except frankfurters, and bring to the boil. Simmer for 2-2½ hours or until all the ingredients are tender. Remove bones and bay leaves and cut meat into strips or cubes. Purée the rest of the ingredients, if preferred. Add meat and sliced frankfurters and reheat soup.

Makes 8-10 servings

HINT
* Place beans in a large saucepan and cover with cold water. Cook for 5 minutes on high heat. Remove from heat, cover with lid, and soak for 1 hour.

# Supreme potato soup

Rich and tasty!

   6 potatoes, peeled and diced
   2 onions, finely chopped
   1 stalk celery, chopped
   750 ml hot chicken stock
   50 ml butter
   50 ml cake flour
   500 ml hot milk
   3 ml prepared mustard
   salt and freshly ground black pepper to taste
   ½ x 410 g tin whole tomatoes, coarsely chopped
   10 ml dried or 30 ml chopped fresh parsley
   50 g Cheddar cheese, grated (125 ml)
   juice of ½ lemon

Simmer potatoes, onions and celery in hot stock for 15 minutes or until tender. Melt butter in a separate saucepan, stir in flour, then add hot milk and prepared mustard. Stir until thickened. Season with salt and pepper. Add white sauce to potato mixture along with tomatoes. Add remaining ingredients and heat through.

Makes 4 servings

# All-in-one-pot vegetable soup

This soup is cooked in a pressure cooker. The cooker should not be filled more than halfway, and the pressure should drop to 0 before removing the lid.

> 500 g sliced beef shin
> 100 g split peas (125 ml)
> 1 litre water
> salt and freshly ground black pepper to taste
> 2 onions, chopped
> 2 cloves garlic, crushed
> 1½ x 115 g tins tomato paste
> 5 ml brown sugar
> 2 carrots, diced
> 2 stalks soup celery, sliced
> 300 g green beans, sliced (500 ml)
> 5 ml dried or 15 ml chopped fresh mixed herbs
> 30 ml Worcester sauce

Place meat, peas, water, salt, pepper, onions and garlic in pressure cooker. Heat slowly to 50 kPa pressure and maintain pressure for 35-40 minutes. Add tomato paste, brown sugar, carrots, celery and green beans and simmer for a further 30-40 minutes. Remove shin bones (which should have separated from the meat by this time) and cut meat into small pieces. Mash some of the vegetables, if preferred. Season soup with mixed herbs and Worcester sauce and simmer for a few minutes.

Makes 6 servings

**TO TAKE ALONG:** Grated Parmesan cheese and a slice of flavoured bread (for example Traveller's loaf, p. 47).

---

VARIATION
* The meat, onions and garlic may be fried beforehand in 30 ml cooking oil.

---

# Sweetpepper soup

You might as well take two servings along to the office, because everyone will want to sample this soup and beg for the recipe. Use red sweet peppers only – not the green variety.

> 6 red sweet peppers, seeded and cut into strips
> 1 pear, peeled and cubed
> 3 carrots, grated
> 2 onions, sliced
> 1 large potato, peeled and grated
> 2 cloves garlic, crushed
> 30 ml olive or cooking oil
> 30 ml cake flour
> salt, Tabasco sauce and cayenne pepper to taste
> 1,5 litres chicken stock
> 15 ml lemon juice
> 5 ml grated lemon rind
> 1 x 61 g tin tomato paste

Fry sweet peppers, pear, carrots, onions, potato and garlic in oil. Sprinkle with flour. Season with salt, Tabasco sauce and cayenne pepper to taste. Add stock, lemon juice and rind and bring to the boil. Add tomato paste and simmer for 30-40 minutes. Process soup in a food processor until smooth. Heat through.

Makes 6-8 servings

**TO TAKE ALONG:** 1 white process cheese cube for adding to each serving of soup, cheese and onion muffins (p. 61) or, to make it even more special, sour cream for spooning on top of the soup just before eating it.

---

VARIATION
* If the soup is to be eaten at home, garnish it as follows: Grill an additional sweet pepper in the oven until the skin turns black and blistery. Allow to sweat in a plastic bag for 30 minutes, cool and pull off the skin. Cut the sweet pepper into thin strips and arrange on top of the soup, along with a dollop of sour cream.

---

# Trix's quick gazpacho

(A traditional Spanish soup)

Spanish muleteers often make gazpacho at the roadside. The garlic is crushed with a little salt and oil between two stones, and then rubbed over the inside of an earthenware dish. Cucumbers and tomatoes are finely shredded and layered in the dish, often accompanied by breadcrumbs and olive oil. The earthenware dish is then wrapped in a wet cloth and left in the sun. When the cloth is dry, the soup is ready. Admittedly, Trix's soup is not the real thing, but may be even tastier!

  1 x 410 g tin tomato soup
  2 x 200 ml tins tomato cocktail
  1½ stalks celery, chopped
  ¼-½ small English cucumber (187,5 ml), chopped
  1 onion, finely chopped
  1 clove garlic, crushed
  ½ avocado, peeled and cubed (125 ml)
  ½ green sweet pepper, seeded and chopped
     (62,5 ml)
  10 ml dried or 30 ml chopped fresh parsley
  37,5 ml wine vinegar
  25 ml olive oil
  salt and freshly ground black pepper to taste
  2,5 ml Worcester sauce
  Tabasco sauce to taste

Mix all the ingredients. Cover and refrigerate overnight. Pour into 6 flasks and try to keep in a cool place until eaten.

Makes 8 servings

**TO TAKE ALONG:** Slices of French bread with garlic butter.

# Chilled cucumber soup

A refreshing chilled soup to take away in a flask or jug on a hot summer's day.

  1 English cucumber, cubed
  900 ml chicken stock
  1 medium onion, chopped
  1 clove garlic, crushed
  salt and freshly ground black pepper to taste
  30 ml butter
  40 ml cake flour
  25 ml lemon juice
  2 small egg yolks
  175 ml thin cream
  chopped fresh mint for garnishing (optional)

Cook cucumber, stock, onion and garlic together for about 20 minutes. Allow to cool, then liquidise. Season with salt and pepper. Melt butter, add flour and stir-fry lightly. Gradually stir cucumber purée into the flour mixture. Bring to the boil, stirring continuously, and simmer for 2 minutes. Add lemon juice. Mix egg yolks and cream and add a little soup. Pour egg mixture into saucepan. Heat through, beating continuously, but do not allow to boil. Allow to cool and adjust seasoning, if necessary. Sprinkle with mint.

Makes 4 servings

**TO TAKE ALONG:** Egg or cheese sandwich.

HINT
* Conservative eaters who are wary of chilled soups will be happy to know that this soup is just as delicious served hot.

# Sandwiches, fillings and spreads

## HINTS FOR MAKING SANDWICHES

### Bread

* It's easier to slice bread that has been refrigerated for a few hours.
* A bread knife should have a saw-toothed blade.
* One loaf makes about 28 slices.
* The following are suitable sandwich bases: brown, whole-wheat, white, rye, fruit or nut loaves, rolls (brown, whole-wheat or white), pita breads and even toast.
* Combine a slice of brown bread with a slice of white.
* If the slices are very thin a third slice may be added, e.g. a slice of rye bread between 2 white slices.

### Butter

* Butter must be soft and spreadable.
* Flavoured butters (p. 18) may also be used as spreads.
* If the filling is also spreadable, butter only one side of a slice of bread.

### Filling

* If the filling is very moist, don't make sandwiches too long in advance, otherwise the bread will become soggy.

*Bread and fillings: bully beef spread (p. 32), egg filling (p. 33) and chicken filling*

* Cover the entire slice of bread with the filling, otherwise the uncovered part will dry out.
* Prepare fillings in advance and store in the refrigerator.
* Don't use so much filling that it runs out at the sides of the sandwich.

### Finishing

* Using a sharp knife, cut sandwiches into desired shapes.
* Using a biscuit cutter, cut out fun shapes for toddlers.
* Wrap sandwiches in waxed paper, greaseproof paper, aluminium foil, plastic or clingwrap.

## SANDWICH FILLINGS

### Meat fillings

* Cold, finely cut or flaked beef, lamb, pork or chicken moistened with salad dressing, prepared mustard or mustard sauce, chutney (e.g. tomato or banana and raisin chutney, p. 16) or tomato sauce.
* Cold sliced beef, lamb, pork or chicken marinated in French salad dressing, with salad ingredients.
* Cold bobotie with chutney and sliced banana.
* Grated biltong moistened with a little prepared mustard.
* Sliced biltong marinated in French salad dressing (p. 66).
* Sliced ham and banana sprinkled with lemon juice.
* Chopped Vienna sausages mixed with prepared mustard and mayonnaise.
* Finely chopped ham mixed with chopped canned

pineapple and mayonnaise.

* Liver pâté and tomato.
* Liver pâté mixed with grilled bacon pieces and grated cheese, moistened with mayonnaise and covered with lettuce.
* Flaked (or sliced) leftover chicken or turkey, sliced cucumber and sandwich spread. (Crumbled blue cheese may be added to sandwich spread.)
* Finely chopped chicken, finely chopped almonds and sandwich spread with lettuce.
* Thinly sliced frankfurters or boerewors with mustard (sauce or prepared mustard).
* Corned beef and gherkins moistened with mayonnaise and flavoured with chutney and chopped chives.

# Biltong spread

This meat filling will keep in the refrigerator for a few days. Use it in sandwiches with sliced cucumber or gherkins, or even as a Snackwich filling.

    125 g smooth cream cheese with chives
    30 ml mayonnaise
    30 ml lemon juice
    30 ml chopped fresh parsley
    60 g shredded biltong (120 ml)
    salt and black pepper to taste

Combine all the ingredients.

# Bully beef spread

This meat filling will keep in the refrigerator for a few days. Spread chutney on the bread before adding the filling.

    1 x 300 g tin bully beef, mashed
    100 g cucumber, finely chopped
    30 ml chopped chives

    50 ml mayonnaise
    5 ml lemon juice

Combine all the ingredients.

# Curried chicken filling

Use this filling with lettuce.

    250 ml cold cooked chicken, flaked
    15 ml mayonnaise
    1 ml mild curry powder
    5 ml chutney
    a few drops Tabasco sauce

Combine all the ingredients.

# Tongue spread

Reserve a little of the liquid in which the tongue was cooked and add it to the tongue in the food processor to facilitate the process. Use as a sandwich spread and with biscuits, Melba toast (p. 25) or crudités (p. 72).

    500 g cooked tongue, finely chopped
    15 ml lemon juice
    30 ml chopped chives
    30 ml chopped capers (optional)
    5 ml prepared mustard
    100 ml thick cream
    30-50 ml mayonnaise
    ½ stalk celery, chopped

Place all the ingredients in a food processor and process until smooth. Spoon the spread into small, individual pâté dishes.

Sufficient for 10 small dishes

---

VARIATION
* Add 15 ml brandy to ingredients in food processor and process.

## How to cook a tongue

Cover tongue with cold water. Add 5 ml salt for each litre of water if the tongue is fresh. (Do not add salt to pickled tongue.) Add a few black peppercorns or whole allspice and 1 or 2 bay leaves tied in a muslin bag. (Fresh herbs such as sprigs of parsley, thyme or rosemary may also be added.) Add 1 or 2 carrots, 1 large onion and 1 turnip to the tongue. Bring to the boil, reduce heat and simmer until tender: 3-4 hours for ox tongue and 1-2 hours for sheep's tongue. Remove tongue from saucepan and immerse in cold water immediately to loosen the skin. Remove the skin and use as required. It is delicious on bread with mustard or mustard sauce, in a salad or simply spread with mustard and rolled up.

## Egg fillings

* Scrambled eggs mixed with a little mayonnaise and a dash of tomato sauce or scrambled eggs and sliced tomato.
* Finely chopped hard-boiled egg mixed with crisply fried bacon and moistened with a little salad dressing or mayonnaise.
* Mashed hard-boiled egg mixed with prepared mustard.
* Hard-boiled egg slices, sliced cucumber and sandwich spread.

## Club sandwiches with egg

60 ml mayonnaise or chutney
12 thin slices white bread, lightly toasted if preferred
8 lettuce leaves
250 g bacon, fried
4 hard-boiled eggs, sliced
3 tomatoes, sliced
½ English cucumber, sliced
salt and freshly ground black pepper

Spread mayonnaise or chutney on all the slices of bread. Place lettuce leaves on 4 slices, followed by about half the bacon, eggs, tomatoes and cucumber. Season with salt and pepper. Cover each slice of bread with another slice. Repeat filling and cover with remaining slices of bread. Cut club sandwiches into triangles.

Makes 4 servings

## Egg filling with sunflower seeds and ham

Sunflower seeds provide an interesting texture variation.

1 hard-boiled egg, chopped
7 ml mayonnaise
1 ml dry mustard
1 clove garlic, crushed
10 ml sunflower seeds, toasted (optional)
1 slice ham, cubed

Combine all the ingredients.

## Egg filling with capers

Use with lettuce leaves on lightly toasted bread.

4 hard-boiled eggs, finely chopped
30 ml mayonnaise
15 ml capers
60 ml sour cream
10 ml dried or 30 ml chopped fresh parsley
salt and freshly ground black pepper to taste

Combine all the ingredients.

## Cheese fillings

* Cottage/cream cheese mixed with one of the following: honey, tomato sauce, fish paste, vegetable extract, chopped egg, savoury cooked mince, chopped onion and pickles, pieces of glacé ginger.
* Cottage cheese mixed with grated cheese, chopped radish and cucumber or gherkins and mayonnaise.
* Cheese slices with chutney and celery.
* Grated cheese, mayonnaise and/or tomato sauce.
* Cheese slice, cold meat and mustard (prepared or mustard sauce) with lettuce.
* Cream cheese mixed with chopped nuts, salted peanuts and chopped raisins. Add a few drops of lemon or orange juice.
* Grated cheese mixed with sandwich spread, with a lettuce leaf.
* Crumbled blue cheese mixed with sandwich spread.
* Chunky cottage cheese (plain or savoury) mixed with sandwich spread, with a slice of salami (especially on rye bread).
* Slices of mozzarella cheese, salami and tomato on rye bread. Cucumber and a sprig of fresh basil will add a nice touch.
* Chunky cottage cheese and sliced fresh fruit, such as apples (dipped in lemon juice), clingstone peaches or even grapes. Scatter poppy seeds over fruit.
* Goat's milk cheese slices, beetroot slices, a few onion rings and lettuce. Sprinkle lightly with olive oil, sunflower seeds and pepper.

## Grated cheese and bacon filling

200 g Cheddar cheese, grated (500 ml)
4 rashers rindless bacon, shredded and crisply fried
1 ml prepared mustard
20 ml chutney

Combine all the ingredients.

## Blue-cheese and apple spread

This filling is delicious on rye bread.

1 apple
10 ml lemon juice
50 g blue cheese, crumbled (100 ml)
25 ml mayonnaise
3 ml dry mustard
4 slices cold leg of pork

Grate apple, sprinkle with lemon juice and drain well. Mix apple with remaining ingredients, except meat. Spoon onto rye bread and add a slice of meat.

## Cottage cheese and beef filling

Combine filling with a slice of cold cooked beef on bread.

125 g smooth cottage cheese
15 ml chutney
salt and freshly ground black pepper to taste
a few drops Tabasco sauce
1 gherkin, chopped
4 slices cooked beef

Combine all the ingredients, except meat.

## Cheese and raisin filling

A welcome change from the usual sandwich fillings.

100 g Edam or Cheddar cheese, grated (250 ml)
15-25 ml seedless raisins
15 ml mayonnaise

Combine all the ingredients.

# Pear and ricotta sandwich filling

Bored with the usual sandwich fillings? Try this one – this pear and ricotta filling is refreshingly different and delicious on rye bread.

    125 g ricotta cheese
    30 ml sherry
    7,5 ml boiling water
    slices of rye bread
    a few pear slices, sprinkled with lemon juice
    toasted, chopped walnuts
    lettuce leaves

Mix cheese, sherry and boiling water and spread on a slice of bread. Arrange pear slices, sprinkled with lemon juice, on top. Scatter toasted, chopped walnuts over pear slices and top with lettuce leaves. Cover with a second slice of bread.

## Fruit and vegetable fillings

* Drained asparagus salad cuts moistened with mayonnaise and mustard.
* Avocado mashed with lemon juice and moistened with sour cream, with a slice of ham or smoked salmon.
* Grilled brinjal and sweet pepper slices on rye bread with grated Parmesan cheese.
* Grilled baby marrow and brinjal slices with marinated sun-dried tomatoes.
* Avocado, grated onion and lemon juice, moistened with mayonnaise or cottage cheese, if preferred.
* Sliced banana, lemon juice and mayonnaise.
* Shredded cabbage, grated carrot and finely chopped onion moistened with mayonnaise or salad dressing.
* Grated carrot moistened with yoghurt (pineapple or granadilla) and topped with a sprinkling of sunflower seeds.
* Leftover vegetables mixed with chopped onion and moistened with mayonnaise or cottage cheese.
* Sliced banana, crisply fried bacon and lettuce leaves.

# Avocado and bacon spread

With this avocado and bacon filling the bread need not be buttered. If stored, lightly cover the surface of the spread with clingwrap.

    125 g rindless bacon, chopped and crisply fried
    1 ripe avocado, mashed
    10 ml grated onion
    ¼ or ½ clove garlic, crushed
    salt and freshly ground black pepper to taste
    10 ml lemon juice
    15-25 ml mayonnaise

Combine all the ingredients.

# Sandwich spread

Sandwich spread may be used on its own, or otherwise to pep up other fillings, especially egg- or cheese-based ones.

    1 English cucumber, grated and drained
    1 onion, finely chopped
    3 carrots, grated
    1 large red sweet pepper, chopped
    1 large green sweet pepper, chopped
    white vinegar to cover vegetables
    about 500 ml mayonnaise

Place the cucumber, onion, carrots and sweet peppers in a dish suitable for marinating, cover with vinegar and leave overnight. Drain vegetables well and mix with mayonnaise.

# Brinjal spread

The first time I tasted this spread I wasn't quite sure what it was. It was so delicious, however, that I begged for the recipe and discovered, to my utter astonishment, that brinjal was the main ingredient.

1 large brinjal
½ small onion, finely chopped
175 ml fresh white breadcrumbs
30 ml plain yoghurt
2 cloves garlic, crushed
100 ml chopped fresh parsley
15 ml wine or cider vinegar
20 ml lemon juice
100 ml olive oil
salt and freshly ground black pepper to taste

Bake brinjal at 180 ˚C for 1 hour. Remove from oven and allow to cool. Pull off skin and chop pulp finely. Add remaining ingredients and process in a food processor until smooth. Leave overnight.

Makes 500 ml spread

**TO TAKE ALONG:** Spread slices of French bread thinly with garlic butter and grill in a heated griddle pan or under the oven grill. Allow to cool and pack together with brinjal spread.

# Fish fillings

* Lemon butter, fish paste, grated cheese and chopped gherkins.
* Mashed sardines mixed with cayenne pepper, hard-boiled egg and lemon butter and/or mayonnaise.
* Salmon, haddock or other processed fish mixed with chopped hard-boiled egg and chopped pickles and moistened with salad dressing and/or mayonnaise.
* Cooked flaked fish mixed with chopped cucumber and moistened with tomato sauce and a little mayonnaise.
* Flaked smoked snoek mixed with chopped gherkins and moistened with cottage cheese and/or mayonnaise.
* Tuna and gherkins moistened with mayonnaise or cream cheese.
* Flaked smoked snoek or angelfish and chopped onion, moistened with sandwich spread.
* Sardines, onion and sliced tomato.
* Cooked mashed fish cake with mayonnaise, sandwich spread or chutney and lettuce.

# Tuna filling

Also use with lettuce in a hot dog roll.

1 x 185 g tin tuna, drained and flaked
½ onion, chopped
30 ml mayonnaise
15 ml tomato sauce
15 ml chutney
4 gherkins, chopped (optional)

Combine all the ingredients.

# Shrimp and cream cheese spread

Use on sandwiches with avocado slices and onion rings.

250 g cooked shrimps, shelled
200 g cream cheese with chives (200 ml)
20 ml lemon juice

Combine all the ingredients.

*Stuffed bread (p. 39)*

# STUFFED BREADS AND ROLLS

## Basic hamburger

The hamburger will always remain the all-time favourite, and small wonder – it's delicious fun food for the young and not-so-young, the ideal takeaway meal and even suitable for entertaining.

> 250 g lean minced pork
> 250 g lean minced beef
> 1 thick slice bread, soaked in 125 ml milk
> 1 medium onion, chopped
> salt and freshly ground black pepper to taste
> 6 hamburger buns or pita breads
> lettuce
> sliced tomato and cucumber

Lightly blend mince, bread and onion, using a fork. Season. Shape round, flat patties and shallow-fry for 7-10 minutes on each side (or until done), or grill them over the coals, under a preheated oven grill or in a griddle pan. Allow to cool and assemble hamburgers with buns, lettuce leaves and tomato and cucumber slices.

Makes 6 servings

**TO TAKE ALONG:** Cold ginger yoghurt sauce consisting of 175 ml sour cream or plain yoghurt, grated rind of ½ lemon, 30 ml lemon juice, 30 ml honey, 15 ml chopped fresh ginger root and salt and pepper to taste.

### HINTS
* Spread mustard sauce, chutney (see tomato or banana and raisin chutney, p. 16) on buns before making hamburgers.
* Spread flavoured butter on buns.
* Use white, whole-wheat or round brown rolls, pita bread, 2 slices of toast, griddlecake or fresh potbread as hamburger bases.

### VARIATIONS
* **Flavoursome hamburgers:** Add 10 ml soy sauce and 30 ml dry sherry to basic mixture.
* **Hamburgers with carrot:** 3 drops Tabasco sauce, 1 carrot, grated, and 10 ml dried or 30 ml chopped fresh parsley.
* **Hamburgers with apple:** 1 ml grated nutmeg, 5 ml ground coriander, 1 green-skinned apple, grated and drained, 15 ml lemon juice and 1 crushed clove garlic.
* **Hamburgers with mustard:** 5 ml dried or 15 ml chopped fresh parsley, 15 ml lemon juice and 15 ml prepared mustard.
* Replace or complement the lettuce, sliced tomato and cucumber with fried or raw onion slices, gherkins, pineapple slices, cheese slices, young spinach leaves, avocado slices, mushroom slices and grilled baby marrow or brinjal slices.

### How to shape hamburger patties

Hamburger patties are usually round and 15-25 mm thick. Shape the patties between the palms of your hands, then press to flatten them. Alternatively, shape a square on a sheet of waxed paper and cut out circles using a biscuit cutter, glass or empty tin. Plastic moulds for shaping patties are also available. Refrigerate patties for 30 minutes before use – cover lightly with waxed paper to prevent them from drying out.

### How to freeze uncooked hamburger patties

Pack the hamburger patties in an airtight plastic bag or container. Stack the patties, but separate the layers with Foilene. In airtight packaging hamburger patties can be frozen for up to 3 months.

### How to add interest to hamburger patties

* After preparing the hamburger patties, sprinkle them with freshly ground black pepper.
* Press uncooked patties into coarse salt and grill them.
* Prepare a flavoured butter, e.g. mushroom butter, then freeze and slice it (see flavoured butters, p. 18). Shape hamburger patties around slices of flavoured butter.
* Shape patties around slices of hard-boiled egg or cheese.
* Grate hard cheese into the meat mixture and serve as cheeseburgers.
* Sandwich two thin meat patties together with the following filling: Mix and refrigerate 200 g blanched and chopped spinach, 125 ml cottage cheese, 1 crushed clove garlic, 1 chopped onion and 5 ml lemon juice.

# Giant beef salad sandwich

Use leftover, preferably rare, beef.

> 500 g cold cooked Scotch fillet
> 5 ml paprika
> 2 ml dry mustard
> salt and freshly ground black pepper to taste
> 1 clove garlic, crushed
> 25 ml olive oil
> 15 ml dry red wine or wine vinegar
> 2-3 gherkins, chopped
> black olives
> French or round bread

Cut meat into strips. Mix seasonings, garlic, oil and wine or vinegar and sprinkle over meat. Marinate meat for 1 hour. Drain meat and mix with gherkins and olives. Halve loaf, hollow it out slightly and spoon in filling. Cut bread into wedges.

Makes 6-8 servings

```
VARIATIONS
*  First spread halved bread with flavoured butter, such as
   garlic butter.
*  Sprinkle meat with French salad dressing instead of vine-
   gar and oil.
```

# Stuffed bread

The ideal bread for taking along to an office function. Take along a small jar of mustard sauce.

> 1 French bread
> 500 g ham, polony or luncheon meat, thinly sliced
> lettuce leaves, well rinsed and dried
>
> HERBED BUTTER
> 90 g butter (100 ml)
> 15 ml dried or 50 ml chopped fresh herbs

> 12,5 ml prepared mustard
> 10 ml lemon juice
> salt and freshly ground black pepper to taste

First mix ingredients for herbed butter. Slice bread, but do not cut all the way through – it should remain in one piece, almost like a concertina. Spread herbed butter between slices. Fold meat slices in half and place between bread slices. Add a lettuce leaf to each slice of meat. Wrap bread in aluminium foil (shiny side in) or clingwrap for taking along to the office or a picnic.

Makes 6 servings

```
VARIATION
*  Add a slice of tomato and cheese of your choice to
   each meat slice when stuffing the bread.
```

# Stuffed French bread

Serve this bread as a snack or pack it in a lunch box or picnic basket.

> 1 long French bread
> 250 g butter (270 ml)
> 150 g salami, cubed
> 150 g ham, cubed
> 1 green sweet pepper, cubed
> 4 gherkins, sliced
> salt and pepper to taste

Hollow out the French bread on the inside, leaving a crust of about 1 cm all round. Crumble the bread that has been removed and combine with remaining ingredients. Stuff the hollowed-out bread with this mixture. Wrap the bread tightly in aluminium foil or clingwrap and refrigerate overnight. Transport the bread in its covering. Slice carefully when needed, and serve.

Makes 1 bread

# Bread wheels

A mouthwatering snack, or an extra treat in the lunch box.

> 8 slices white bread, crusts removed
> 1-2 avocados, mashed
> salt and freshly ground black pepper to taste
> 1 clove garlic, crushed
> 20 ml sour cream
> 15 ml lemon juice
> 8 slices ham or smoked salmon

Roll a rolling pin over slices of bread to make them thinner. Cover with a damp cloth. Mix avocado, salt, pepper, garlic, sour cream and lemon juice. Spread each slice with avocado mixture and top with ham or salmon. Halve slices and roll up, starting at short side. Wrap each roll in clingwrap. Refrigerate for about 2 hours or until firm. Cut each roll into about 5 slices.

Makes 4-6 servings

# Bread wheels with tongue filling

> 50 g mushrooms, chopped
> 1 small onion, chopped
> 15 ml cooking oil
> 250 g cooked corned tongue, minced
> 75 ml cream or mayonnaise
> 5 ml prepared mustard
> freshly ground black pepper to taste
> 1 day-old white bread

Sauté mushrooms and onion in heated oil. Mix thoroughly with remaining ingredients, except bread. Slice bread thinly and remove crusts. Using a rolling pin, flatten slices slightly. Spread filling evenly on each slice. Roll up each slice separately, as you would a Swiss roll, and wrap in clingwrap. Refrigerate for 1 hour. Remove clingwrap and

*Fillings for pancakes, potatoes and vetkoek: savoury mince with tomato (p. 42) and chicken liver filling (back)*

cut into 5 mm thick wheels.

Makes 12 servings

HINT
* To pack the bread wheels for an office party, rejoin them in the shape of the original roll and wrap in clingwrap.

# FILLINGS FOR PANCAKES, POTATOES, PUFFS, VETKOEK AND ROULADES

## Chicken liver filling

> 125 g rindless bacon, coarsely chopped
> 1 onion, chopped
> 1 clove garlic, crushed
> ½ green sweet pepper, seeded and chopped
> cooking oil (optional)
> 250 g chicken livers, coarsely chopped
> 2 large tomatoes, skinned and coarsely chopped
> 100 ml dry white wine or chicken stock
> 2 ml dried or 5 ml chopped fresh basil
> 2 ml dried or 5 ml chopped fresh origanum
> salt and freshly ground black pepper to taste
> pinch sugar

Fry bacon until crisp. Remove from pan and set aside. Sauté onion, garlic and sweet pepper in the same pan until onion is translucent. Replenish rendered fat with oil, if necessary. Add chicken livers to onion mixture and fry until brown. Add tomatoes and wine or stock and simmer until livers are done. Add seasonings.

Sufficient for 6-7 pancakes or 6 potatoes

VARIATION
* For a creamier filling, add a little cream or sour cream.

# Savoury mince with tomato

500 g mince
30 ml cooking oil
1 large onion, chopped
1 clove garlic, crushed
1 x 410 g tin tomatoes, chopped
5 ml brown sugar
2 ml dried or 5 ml chopped fresh basil
3 ml dried or 10 ml chopped fresh thyme
salt and freshly ground black pepper to taste

Fry mince in heated oil until it changes colour. Add onion and garlic and sauté until onion is translucent. Add tomatoes, brown sugar and seasonings and simmer for about 10 minutes. Allow to cool.

HINTS
* Combine mince filling with a flavoured white sauce and use to fill pita breads or bouchées.
* Use as a filling for baked potatoes. Sprinkle cheese on top.
* Bake small pancakes and stack 3-5 with the filling in between, to make an individual serving that can be taken away and reheated. Top with a white sauce or cheese sauce.
* Hollow out parcooked baby marrows or use a hollowed-out tomato or sweet pepper. Drain vegetables and spoon savoury mince into hollows. Top with a little cheese sauce or flavoured white sauce, or simply sprinkle with grated cheese. Pack and reheat at the office.

# Curried mince

500 g mince
30 ml cooking oil
1 large onion, chopped
1 clove garlic, crushed
15 ml mild curry powder
15 ml turmeric
salt and freshly ground black pepper to taste
15 ml vinegar
15 ml chutney
3 ml brown sugar
1 ml ground ginger
1 cinnamon stick
100 ml hot meat stock

Fry mince in heated oil until it changes colour. Add onion and garlic and sauté until onion is translucent. Add curry powder and turmeric and fry for a few minutes. Add salt, pepper, vinegar, chutney, brown sugar, ginger, cinnamon stick and stock and simmer for about 10 minutes. Allow meat mixture to cool. Remove cinnamon stick.

HINTS
* Use with banana and chutney in pita bread.
* Use to fill vetkoek.
* Use to fill vegetables.
* Use with chutney in pancakes.

## MORE FILLINGS FOR BAKED POTATOES (p. 95)

* **Creamed spinach filling** (see pancake filling, right).
* **Mushroom sauce:** Fry 250 g fresh sliced mushrooms in 50 g butter. Combine 1 packet mushroom soup powder, 1 x 170 g tin evaporated milk and 375 ml water or milk (or ½ milk and ½ water). Add to mushrooms and simmer for a few minutes. Add 30-50 ml sherry.

## MORE FILLINGS FOR PUFFS (p. 90)

* **Snoek filling:** Combine 250 g flaked smoked snoek, 125 g smooth cottage cheese with chives, 125 ml mayonnaise, 30 ml lemon juice, salt, cayenne pepper and freshly ground black pepper to taste.
* **Ham filling:** Combine 350 g diced ham, 50 ml chopped fresh parsley, freshly ground black pepper to taste, 5 ml prepared mustard, 10 ml lemon juice and 100 ml mayonnaise.
* **Bacon filling:** Fry 250 g coarsely chopped rindless bacon until crisp, then drain. Fry 125 g sliced mushrooms in bacon fat and butter. Add 1 chopped onion and sauté until translucent. Add 25 g cake flour and stir-fry for 1 minute. Add 125 ml milk, 100 ml cream and 2 ml dried or 5 ml chopped fresh mint. Stir until cooked and thickened. Add bacon and 125 ml cooked peas.
* **Tuna filling:** Hard-boil 2 eggs and allow to cool. Chop eggs, 1 small onion and 1 slice whole-wheat bread together finely. Add 50 ml each cream cheese and mayonnaise, 2 x 200 g tins drained tuna and salt and black pepper. Mix well.

## MORE SNACKWICH FILLINGS

* **Chicken and cheese filling:** Combine 200 g cooked flaked chicken, 1 chopped onion, 100 g grated Cheddar cheese and 2 beaten egg yolks.
* **Bacon and onion filling:** Fry 250 g rindless streaky bacon, coarsely chopped, and 1 chopped onion until bacon is crisp. Add 30 ml cake flour and stir over heat until golden brown. Add 50 ml milk and 15 ml cream and heat until slightly thickened. Allow to cool. Stir in 15 ml grated Parmesan cheese, if preferred.
* **Ham and cheese filling:** Chop 125 g ham coarsely. Add 100 g grated Cheddar cheese (250 ml), 15 ml grated onion, 1 skinned chopped tomato, black pepper to taste and 30 ml mayonnaise. Mix well. Stir in 6 pitted olives, chopped (optional).

* **Spinach and cheese filling:** Sauté 6 chopped spring onions and 2 crushed cloves garlic in 5 ml butter. Remove from heat and add 250 g chopped fresh spinach (stalks removed and blanched), pinch nutmeg, 50 ml cottage cheese and 50 ml chopped fresh parsley.

## ANOTHER FILLING FOR A ROULADE (p. 72)

* **Asparagus filling:** Combine 2 hard-boiled eggs, finely chopped, 60 ml mayonnaise, 50 ml sour cream, 1 x 410 g tin asparagus salad cuts, drained, and 100 ml grated Cheddar cheese.

## MORE PANCAKE FILLINGS (p. 52)

* **Vegetable filling:** Lightly stir-fry vegetables in season in garlic butter so that they remain crisp and firm.
* **Spinach filling:** Use shop-bought creamed spinach or prepare it yourself: Slowly heat 600 g drained cooked spinach, 100 ml thick fresh cream, 15 ml cake flour, 1 chopped and sautéed onion and 1 clove garlic. Stir continuously until sauce thickens. Season with salt and pepper. Add 125 g crumbled feta cheese and 3 rashers bacon, chopped and fried until crisp. Sprinkle grated cheese over folded pancake, if preferred.
* **Cold ham filling:** Combine 250 g ham, cut into strips, 15 ml chopped fresh parsley, 50 ml mayonnaise, 50 ml plain yoghurt, freshly ground black pepper to taste and 5 ml whole-grain mustard, or: Add 200 g chopped ham and 250 ml grated Cheddar cheese to white sauce (see tuna filling below). Season to taste.
* **Tuna filling:** Melt 60 g butter, then stir in 60 ml cake flour. Stir in 325 ml hot milk and keep on stirring until thickened. Add 1 x 200 g tin drained tuna, 1 chopped and sautéed onion, 100 g grated Cheddar cheese (250 ml) and 30 ml chopped fresh parsley.
* **Breakfast pancake:** Sliced banana, muesli, yoghurt and honey.
* Snoek filling (above left) or biltong spread (p. 32).
* Custard filling.
* Flavoursome mince filling, e.g. curried mince (p. 42).
* Leftover meat with cheese sauce.
* Curried chicken filling (p. 32).
* Vienna sausage and tomato and onion mix or mustard sauce.

# Sandwich substitutes

## Pumpkin and cinnamon loaf

This sweet, moist loaf is delicious with butter, but just as tasty without.

  210 g cake flour (450 ml)
  2,5 ml baking powder
  5 ml bicarbonate of soda
  2 ml salt
  2,5 ml cinnamon
  60 ml pecan nuts or walnuts, chopped
  50 ml seedless raisins (optional)
  60 g butter
  160 g sugar (200 ml)
  2 eggs, beaten
  5 ml vanilla essence
  250 g well-drained cooked pumpkin or butternut,
    mashed
  87,5 ml milk

Sift dry ingredients together. Add nuts and raisins. Cream butter and sugar, then gradually add eggs, beating continuously. Add vanilla essence. Add pumpkin, alternating with flour mixture and milk. Mix thoroughly. Turn into a greased loaf tin and bake at 180 ˚C for 1 hour. Turn out onto a cooling rack.

Makes 1 loaf

## Banana and carrot loaf

This loaf has a cake-like texture and needs no butter at all.

  90 g butter
  200 g brown sugar (250 ml) – not the soft, moist variety
  1 large egg, beaten
  250 ml grated carrot
  250 ml banana pulp
  170 g cake flour (350 ml)
  5 ml bicarbonate of soda
  5 ml cinnamon
  1 ml salt
  50 g walnuts, chopped (125 ml)

Cream butter and sugar until light and creamy. Add egg and mix well. Stir in carrot and banana. Sift dry ingredients together and add to butter and sugar mixture along with nuts. Blend well and turn into a greased, long loaf tin. Bake at 180 ˚C for 1 hour. Allow to cool in tin for 5 minutes, then turn out onto a cooling rack.

Makes 1 loaf

*Almond and cherry loaf (p. 46) and banana and carrot loaf*

HINT
* About 3 medium or 4 small bananas will yield 250 ml pulp.

# Apple loaf

This loaf is as delicious as cake and does not even have to be buttered. Leave the skin intact when grating the apple for this loaf.

>   240 g cake flour (500 ml)
>   pinch salt
>   5 ml bicarbonate of soda
>   115 g butter (125 ml)
>   200 g sugar (250 ml)
>   5 ml vanilla essence
>   2 eggs, beaten
>   25 ml buttermilk or sour milk
>   250 ml grated apple
>   62,5 ml chopped pecan nuts or walnuts (optional)

Sift dry ingredients together. Cream butter and sugar until light and fluffy. Add essence. Gradually add beaten eggs, beating continuously. Add dry ingredients to butter and sugar mixture, alternating with buttermilk and apple and nuts. Blend well. Turn into a greased loaf tin and bake at 180 °C for 1 hour or until a testing skewer comes out clean. Allow to cool in tin for 5 minutes, then turn out onto a cooling rack.

Makes 1 loaf

# Almond cherry loaf

Before adding the cherries, coat them with flour to prevent their sinking to the bottom.

>   3 eggs
>   210 g castor sugar (250 ml)
>   10 drops almond essence
>   2,5 ml vanilla essence
>   500 g self-raising flour (900 ml)
>   3 ml salt
>   100 g halved glacé cherries (160 ml)
>   250 ml milk
>   125 ml cooking oil

Beat eggs until light and creamy. Add castor sugar and continue beating until light. Stir in essences. Sift dry ingredients together, add cherries and stir into egg mixture, alternating with milk and oil. Turn into a greased medium loaf tin and bake at 160 °C for 1½ hours or until golden brown and done. Turn out onto a cooling rack.

VARIATION
*   Replace the cherries with 250 ml fruitcake mixture.

# Handful-of-seeds health loaf

A handful of seeds of your own choice may be added (hence the name). A handful is about 100 ml.

>   600 g Nutty Wheat (4 x 250 ml)
>   10 ml bicarbonate of soda
>   5 ml salt
>   30 ml brown sugar
>   handful of seeds, e.g. sesame, linseed, poppy, toasted
>       sunflower or wheat germ (the latter is not a seed)
>   30 ml cooking oil
>   500 ml buttermilk
>   sesame or poppy seeds for sprinkling (optional)

Sift Nutty Wheat, bicarbonate of soda and salt together. Add husks remaining in sieve to mixture. Add brown sugar and seeds or wheat germ. Stir in oil and buttermilk and mix to a fairly stiff dough. Turn into a greased loaf tin, sprinkle seeds on top and bake at 180 °C for 1 hour. Turn out onto a cooling rack.

Makes 1 loaf

VARIATION
*   Add a grated apple or mashed banana to the dry ingredients along with the liquid.

HINT
* Sunflower seeds should be toasted, otherwise they may react with the bicarbonate of soda and turn green.

# Whole-wheat yeast batter bread

A home-made whole-wheat loaf is always a favourite, especially if no kneading is required!

500 g Nutty Wheat (960 ml)
7 ml salt
30 ml sugar
½ x 10 g packet instant yeast
10 ml honey
65 ml oil
430 ml lukewarm water (see hint)

Combine dry ingredients. Add honey, oil and water and mix to a fairly stiff dough. Place in a greased tin, cover and leave to rise in a warm place until nearly doubled in bulk. Bake at 180 °C for 50 minutes or until done.

Makes 1 loaf

---

VARIATION
* Before baking the bread, sprinkle poppy seeds, linseed or sunflower seeds on top to enhance its appearance.

---

HINT
* The temperature of the water will determine whether the dough will rise or not. If the water is too cold the dough will not rise, and if it's too warm the yeast plant will be destroyed. To obtain the correct temperature, the required amount of water should be made up of one-third boiling water and two-thirds tap water.

# Traveller's loaf

Everyone will be peering into the food basket, eager for another taste of this delicious bread.

1 x 500 g packet self-raising flour (900 ml)
75 g Nutty Wheat (125 ml)
5 ml each dried rosemary, origanum and basil
3 ml ground black pepper
5 ml salt
3 ml seasoning salt
1 large onion, grated
2 cloves garlic, crushed
3 rashers rindless bacon, chopped
15 ml butter
100 g grated Cheddar cheese (250 ml)
about 5 ml Tabasco sauce
500 ml buttermilk
175 ml plain yoghurt
about 50 ml water or milk for rinsing out buttermilk container

Combine dry ingredients. Fry onion, garlic and bacon in heated butter. Add cheese to dry ingredients and mix well. Beat Tabasco sauce, buttermilk and yoghurt together and add to dry ingredients along with fried onion mixture. Rinse buttermilk container out with water or milk, then add liquid to mixture. Mix to a batter. Spoon into a greased loaf tin and bake at 180 °C for 1½ hours or until a testing skewer comes out clean.

Makes 1 loaf

**TO TAKE ALONG:** Soup.

---

VARIATION
* Replace basil with thyme.

---

# Spiral pizza loaf

Knock on the bread with your knuckles: if it sounds hollow, it's done.

   600 g cake flour (750 ml)
   5 ml salt
   7 g instant yeast (10 ml)
   180 ml milk
   60 ml butter
   15 ml sugar
   1 egg, lightly beaten
   75 ml chopped fresh parsley or chives
   melted butter

   FILLING
   1 x 61 g tin tomato paste
   100 g grated Cheddar cheese (250 ml)
   2 cloves garlic, crushed
   10 ml dried or 30 ml chopped fresh origanum

Sift dry ingredients together. Heat milk, butter and sugar until butter has melted and mixture is lukewarm. Add beaten egg and herbs. Add to flour mixture and mix to a dough. Knead until elastic. Leave dough to rest for 10 minutes. Knock down and roll out to form a rectangle. Spread with tomato paste and sprinkle with remaining filling ingredients. Roll up like a Swiss roll and place in a greased 20 x 10 cm loaf tin. Brush with melted butter and allow to rise in a warm place until doubled in bulk. Bake at 180 ˚C for 35 minutes. Brush crust with butter.

Makes 1 loaf

# Home-made pita breads

A batch of these flat, hollow breads in the freezer comes in very handy when you need takeaway meals.

   840 g cake flour (7 x 250 ml)
   10 ml salt
   15 ml sugar
   1 x 10 g packet instant yeast (15 ml)
   25 ml cooking oil
   500 ml lukewarm water
   cake flour for sifting (optional)

Sift flour and salt together. Add sugar and yeast, mixing well. Add oil and water and mix to a soft dough. Knead until smooth and elastic. Cover dough and leave to rise in a warm place until doubled in bulk. Knock down dough and pinch off 16 equal-sized balls. Roll out each ball until about 5 mm thick. Place on a greased baking tray, cover lightly with clingwrap and allow to rise in a warm place for about 20 minutes. Bake at 200 ˚C for 8 minutes or until well puffed up and slightly browned. Turn out onto a cooling rack and allow to cool. Sift flour over, if preferred.

Makes 16 pita breads

**TO TAKE ALONG:** Stuff with salad ingredients, slices of cold leftover meat or a stuffing of your choice.

HINT
* Preheat the baking tray before baking the pita breads. The heat from underneath will ensure a well-puffed-up result.

*Stuffed, home-made pita breads*

# Whole-wheat scones

A delicious variation on the sandwich theme.

1 egg
65 ml cooking oil
about 150 ml milk
140 g self-raising flour (250 ml)
150 g Nutty Wheat (250 ml)
15 ml baking powder
2 ml salt
15 ml castor sugar

Beat egg lightly in a 250 ml measuring cup. Add oil and enough milk to make up 250 ml (about 150 ml milk is required). Sift the dry ingredients together. Return the husks remaining in the sieve to the flour mixture. Add liquid to the dry ingredients and mix to a soft dough. Roll out lightly on a floured surface until about 2 cm thick. Cut out circles with a biscuit cutter. Place on a greased baking tray and bake at 220 °C for 15 minutes or until golden brown.

Makes 8 scones depending on size

---

VARIATIONS
* Replace Nutty Wheat with 280 g self-raising flour (500 ml) for white scones.
* Add 75 g raisins (125 ml) and 100 ml chopped pecan nuts to dry ingredients.
* Add 125 ml chopped dates to dry ingredients.
* **Scone dough wheels with jam and nuts:** Roll out scone dough. Brush with melted butter and jam. Top with sprinkle or chopped nuts. Roll up as you would a Swiss roll and cut into 25 mm thick slices. Place on a greased baking tray and bake at 200 °C for 12-15 minutes.
* **Scone dough wheels with raisin filling:** Roll out scone dough. Brush with melted butter. Sprinkle with 75 g raisins (125 ml), followed by 100 g sugar (125 ml) and 7 ml cinnamon. Roll up as you would a Swiss roll and cut into 25 mm thick slices. Place on a greased baking tray and bake at 200 °C for 12-15 minutes.

---

# Blue-cheese scones

Simply irresistible – whether you like blue cheese or not.

180 g cake flour (375 ml)
15 ml baking powder
3 ml salt
60 g soft butter
60 ml crumbled blue cheese
1 egg, beaten
50-60 ml milk

Sift dry ingredients together. Rub in butter with fingertips until mixture resembles breadcrumbs. Add cheese and mix well. Mix egg and milk. Make a hollow in centre of flour mixture. Using a knife, mix in egg mixture to make a soft dough. Roll out lightly on a floured surface until about 2 cm thick. Cut out circles (4 cm in diameter) with a biscuit cutter. Place on a greased baking tray and bake at 220 °C for 15 minutes or until golden brown. Turn out onto a cooling rack.

Makes 15 scones

# Crumpets

Leftover breakfast crumpets can be buttered immediately and packed in a lunch box.

240 g cake flour (500 ml)
30 ml baking powder
30 ml sugar
5 ml salt
500 ml milk
30 ml cooking oil
2 eggs, beaten

Sift dry ingredients together. Beat remaining ingredients together and add to flour mixture. Mix until smooth. Fry spoonfuls of batter in a greased pan until brown on both sides.

Makes about 30 crumpets

**TO TAKE ALONG:** Grated cheese and jam, syrup or honey.

HINTS
* The batter must have the consistency of thick cream. Add more milk if the batter is too thick.
* Do not turn the crumpets before air bubbles have formed.
* Crumpets that are done must be kept soft by covering them with a clean, dry tea cloth while the rest are being prepared.
* Crumpets can be stacked in pairs, packed in plastic sheets or cling-wrap and frozen for up to 2 months.

# Banana crumpets

These crumpets are just as delicious cold. Sandwich them together with something sweet, such as jam, moskonfyt, honey or syrup.

170 g cake flour (350 ml)
5 ml bicarbonate of soda
5 ml cinnamon
pinch salt
3 eggs, separated
50 ml sugar
150 ml milk
15 ml cooking oil
3 bananas, thinly sliced
50 ml lemon juice

Sift dry ingredients together. Beat egg yolks and sugar together, then add milk and oil. Add dry ingredients to egg mixture, beating until smooth. Sprinkle banana slices with lemon juice and add to mixture. Whisk egg whites until stiff and fold into mixture. Place spoonfuls in a greased, heated pan or frying pan. Brown both sides.

Makes 30 crumpets

# Mealie-meal vetkoek

The mealie meal can be toasted in advance in a heavy-based pan to obtain a deliciously nutty flavour.

170 g cake flour (350 ml)
20 ml baking powder
2 ml salt
60 g mealie meal (125 ml)
25 ml sugar
25 ml butter
250 ml milk
cooking oil for deep-frying

Sift cake flour, baking powder and salt. Add mealie meal and sugar. Rub in butter and combine with milk to form a soft dough. Place spoonfuls of dough in hot oil and fry until golden brown and done.

Makes about 10 vetkoek depending on size

**TO TAKE ALONG:** Curried mince filling (p. 42), savoury mince with tomato (p. 42) or filling of your choice.

HINTS
* The dough should be neither too slack nor too stiff. A stiff dough will inhibit the rising process while a slack dough tends to absorb more oil.
* If the oil is too hot the vetkoek will brown before they are puffed up and done on the inside.
* Fry only a few spoonfuls at a time, otherwise the oil will cool too much and the vetkoek will absorb too much oil.
* Drain the hot vetkoek on paper towelling or crumpled-up brown paper.

## Vetkoek or griddlecakes made with bought bread dough

Buy bread dough from a bakery and use it to make vetkoek or griddlecakes. Leave to rise for about 25 minutes. Knock down the dough and shape into a long roll, about 40 mm in diameter, on a floured surface. Pinch off pieces of about 40 mm and flatten until about 10 mm thick. Leave to rise until doubled in bulk. Shallow- or deep-fry vetkoek until done, and grill griddlecakes over the coals or in a griddle pan.

HINTS
* To ensure a soft surface, cover dough when setting aside to rise.
* Pinch off pieces of dough. Do not cut or tear dough as the gluten will be broken and the elasticity of the dough weakened.

# Whole-wheat vetkoek

Remember to take along an extra clean serviette for handling the vetkoek.

> 390 g Nutty Wheat (750 ml)
> 120 g cake flour (250 ml)
> 20 ml baking powder
> 5 ml salt
> 50 ml golden-brown sugar
> 4 eggs
> 500 ml boiling water
> cooking oil

Combine dry ingredients. Add husks remaining in the sieve to the dry mixture. Beat eggs and gradually stir in boiling water. Add dry ingredients and mix well. Place spoonfuls of batter in hot oil and fry until golden brown and done. Drain on paper towelling.

Makes 16-20 vetkoek

**TO TAKE ALONG:** Biltong spread (p. 32) or snoek filling (p. 43).

# Microwave-and-pan griddlecakes with beer

Even flat beer can be used for this recipe. Allow the beer foam to subside before measuring it out.

> 500 g packet self-raising flour (900 ml)
> 5 ml salt
> 25 ml castor sugar
> 50 ml cooking oil
> 1 x 340 ml bottle or can beer
> cooking oil

Mix dry ingredients. Add oil and beer and mix to a workable dough. Divide dough into 12 equal pieces and shape into balls. Brush with oil, cover with cling-wrap and leave for 10 minutes. Lightly rub or spray oil onto turntable of microwave oven and arrange griddle-cakes around edge. Microwave on 100% power for 6 minutes. Continue grilling in a heated griddle pan until brown on both sides. Allow to cool for takeaway purposes and spread with butter.

Makes 12 griddlecakes

HINTS
* If castor sugar is not available, grind granulated white sugar in a food processor, or place it in a plastic bag and crush it with a rolling pin.
* Use griddlecakes as hamburger bases.
* Use jam and grated cheese as a filling, or a filling of your choice.

# Pancakes

There is nothing quite like a baked pancake, whether dredged with cinnamon sugar or made more substantial with a filling.

> 50 g melted butter (50 ml)
> 120 g cake flour (250 ml)
> pinch salt
> 2 eggs, beaten
> 2 ml salt
> 2 ml sugar
> 250 ml milk
> 80 ml water
> 15 ml vinegar

Using a wire whisk, whisk all the ingredients together until smooth and lump-free. Leave for 30 minutes. Bake thin pancakes.

Makes 12 pancakes

**TO TAKE ALONG:** Cinnamon sugar, one of the fillings in *Sandwiches, fillings and spreads* (pp. 41-42) or a filling of your own choice (p. 43).

VARIATION
* Replace the vinegar with brandy or lemon juice. The latter lends a lighter, softer texture.

HINTS
* If you don't have time to leave the batter for a while, use soda water instead of water. Add the egg yolks to the batter and fold in the stiffly whisked egg whites just before baking the pancakes.
* The more milk you replace with water, the easier it will be to handle the batter and the lighter the pancakes will be.
* Heat the pan well before baking the pancakes. Spatter a few drops of water in the pan to test the heat. If the drops jump around, the pan is hot enough. If they remain motionless, the pan is too cold, and if they evaporate immediately, the pan is too hot.
* The batter and the cooked pancakes can be stored in the refrigerator for 2-3 days.

## How to fold pancakes

* Fold **envelopes** by placing opposite edges of the pancake on the filling.
* Spread the pancakes with a savoury pâté and roll them up tightly. Place the pancakes in the refrigerator or freezer for a few minutes until they are cold and firm. Cut into **wheels**.
* Fold the pancakes in half twice to form **triangles**. Spoon the filling in between the folds.
* Spoon the filling into the centre of each pancake. Press the edges together to form a **parcel**. If a savoury filling is used, tie the parcels with chives that have been immersed in boiling water for a few seconds.
* Spoon a filling onto the pancakes, roll up and fold in half to make a **V-shape**.

# Muffins made easy

## Special muffin mix

As the batter can be refrigerated for 2-3 weeks, you can bake only as many muffins as you need at a time. Vary the flavour of the basic mix by adding ingredients you like, such as coconut or nuts.

    180 g cake flour (375 ml)
    10 ml bicarbonate of soda
    5 ml salt
    260 g whole-wheat flour (500 ml)
    200 g white sugar (250 ml)
    150 g fruitcake mix (250 ml)
    75 g chopped dates (125 ml)
    75 g seedless raisins (125 ml)
    125 ml grated carrot
    2 eggs, beaten
    500 ml milk
    125 ml cooking oil
    5 ml vanilla essence

Sift cake flour, bicarbonate of soda and salt together. Add whole-wheat flour and sugar, mixing well. Blend fruitcake mix, dates, raisins and carrot together, then add to the flour mixture. Mix well. Beat eggs, milk, oil and vanilla essence together. Add to the mixture and blend lightly. The batter may be baked immediately or stored in an airtight container in the refrigerator. Spoon into greased hollows of a muffin pan until two-thirds full. Bake at 200 ˚C for 20-25 minutes. Turn out immediately onto a cooling rack.

Makes 14-16 muffins

*Poppy seed muffins and lemon muffins (p. 57)*

## Poppy seed muffins

A little melted chocolate spooned over the cooled muffins will make them even more special.

    280 g self-raising flour (500 ml)
    15 ml baking powder
    2 ml salt
    50 ml poppy seeds
    140 g white sugar (175 ml)
    100 ml coconut
    1 egg, beaten
    1 ml almond essence
    275 ml milk
    75 ml cooking oil

Sift together flour, baking powder and salt. Add poppy seeds, sugar and coconut. Beat together egg, essence, milk and oil. Add to dry ingredients, blending lightly. Spoon into greased hollows of a muffin pan until two-thirds full. Bake at 200 ˚C for 20 minutes. Turn out onto a cooling rack immediately.

Makes 10 muffins

---

### Baking times in the microwave

Microwave muffins as follows (see also p. 63):

650-700 W microwave oven on 70% power:
2 muffins: 60-90 seconds
4 muffins: 2-3 minutes
6 muffins: 3-5 minutes

800 W microwave oven on 50% power:
2 muffins: 60-90 seconds
4 muffins: 2-3 minutes
6 muffins: 3-5 minutes

# Banana muffins

240 g cake flour (500 ml)
5 ml baking powder
5 ml bicarbonate of soda
5 ml salt
1 ml ground cinnamon
140 g sugar (175 ml)
62,5 ml chopped nuts
about 30 g All-Bran breakfast cereal (250 ml)
1 egg, beaten
120 ml milk
75 ml cooking oil
2 bananas, puréed (about 200 g banana purée) and
    mixed with 15 ml lemon juice

Sift flour, baking powder, bicarbonate of soda, salt and cinnamon together. Add sugar, nuts and All-Bran, mixing well. Beat egg, milk and oil together and add to All-Bran mixture along with banana purée. Mix lightly. Spoon into greased hollows of a muffin pan until two-thirds full. Bake at 200 ˚C for 20-25 minutes. Allow to cool slightly, then turn out onto a cooling rack.

Makes 10 muffins

HINT
* Bananas are available throughout the year. When they are plentiful, freeze them in their skins until needed for baking purposes.

# Banana and chocolate muffins

These muffins will remain moist and delicious, even though they were baked the day before!

240 g cake flour (500 ml)
7 ml baking powder
2,5 ml bicarbonate of soda
2 ml salt
200 g white sugar (250 ml)
60 g butter
125 ml chocolate chips
50 g chopped walnuts (125 ml) (optional)
1 egg, beaten
50 ml milk or buttermilk
2,5 ml vanilla essence
250 ml banana purée (3-4 medium, ripe bananas)

Sift flour, baking powder, bicarbonate of soda and salt together. Add sugar and mix well. Rub in butter until mixture resembles crumbs. Add chocolate chips and walnuts, mixing well. Beat egg, milk and vanilla essence together, then add to flour mixture along with banana purée. Mix lightly. Spoon into greased hollows of a muffin pan until two-thirds full. Bake at 200 ˚C for 25 minutes. Allow to cool slightly, then turn out onto a cooling rack.

Makes 12 large muffins

# Apple muffins

These muffins are so delicious they need no butter at all.

125 g butter
100 g sugar (125 ml)
2 eggs, beaten
125 ml milk
2 ml vanilla essence
½ x 385 g tin pie apples, chopped
140 g self-raising flour (250 ml)
2 ml salt
130 g whole-wheat flour (250 ml)
cinnamon sugar (see hints)

Cream butter and sugar until light and fluffy. Add eggs little by little, beating continuously. Add milk, essence and apples and mix well. Sift self-raising flour and salt together, then add whole-wheat flour. Stir in butter and milk mixture. Mix batter lightly. Spoon into greased hollows of a muffin pan until two-thirds full. Sprinkle with cinnamon sugar. Bake at 200 °C for 20-25 minutes. Leave muffins to cool in pan for 5 minutes, then turn out onto a cooling rack.

Makes 12 muffins

HINTS

* The secret to these muffins lies in creaming the butter and sugar very well.
* Cinnamon sugar is made with about 15 ml ground cinnamon and 300 g sugar (375 ml).

# Date muffins

Dates are wholesome snacks that can even be packed in the lunch box whole.

> 260 g whole-wheat flour (500 ml)
> 250 ml digestive bran
> 15 ml baking powder
> 3 ml salt
> 100 g brown sugar (125 ml)
> 130 g dates, finely cut (200 ml)
> 2 eggs, beaten
> 500 ml milk
> 62,5 ml cooking oil

Mix flour, bran, baking powder and salt. Add brown sugar and dates, mixing well. Beat together eggs, milk and oil and add to mixture. Mix lightly. Spoon into greased hollows of a muffin pan until two-thirds full. Bake at 200 °C for 20 minutes. Turn out onto a cooling rack.

Makes 12 muffins

HINT

* Before cutting up the dates, dip the knife in cake flour to facilitate the process considerably.

# Lemon muffins

> 240 g cake flour (500 ml)
> 15 ml baking powder
> 2 ml salt
> 50 ml coconut
> 140 g sugar (175 ml)
> 5 ml grated lemon rind
> 1 egg, beaten
> 250 ml milk
> 75 ml cooking oil
> 50 ml lemon juice

Sift flour, baking powder and salt together. Add coconut, sugar and rind, mixing well. Beat egg, milk, oil and lemon juice together. Add to flour mixture and mix lightly. Spoon into greased hollows of a muffin pan until two-thirds full. Bake at 200 °C for 20-25 minutes. Turn out onto a cooling rack immediately.

Makes 10 muffins

**TO TAKE ALONG:** Pack whole muffins together with a little butter, a wedge of cheese or a small jar of jam to add to the fun. And don't forget the plastic knife!

HINTS

* To extract the maximum amount of juice from a lemon, place the whole lemon in a preheated oven at 180 °C for 2 minutes. Roll it on a hard surface to soften it slightly, or rinse it under hot water.
* Lemon juice can be frozen in ice trays until needed. Remove the frozen cubes and store them in plastic bags in the freezer.

---

## Spreads for muffins

Butter, grated cheese, jam, honey, syrup and moskonfyt are usually spread on muffins. Sweet muffins are often so tasty that they need no spreads at all. Savoury muffins can be served with a flavoured butter or a meat, vegetable, cheese or fish spread; or try chopped ham, grated biltong or pâté for a delicious treat.

# Cherry Lane muffins

You might as well double the recipe from the start, because these muffins will be much in demand!

   180 g cake flour (375 ml)
   10 ml bicarbonate of soda
   5 ml salt
   125 g whole-wheat flour (250 ml)
   500 ml digestive bran
   250 g seedless raisins (325 ml)
   125 ml chopped pecan nuts or walnuts (optional)
   2 eggs, beaten
   500 ml milk
   125 ml cooking oil
   180 g soft brown sugar (375 ml)
   5 ml vanilla essence
   1 large banana, mashed

Sift cake flour, bicarbonate of soda and salt together. Add whole-wheat flour, bran, raisins and nuts, blending well. Beat eggs, milk, oil, sugar and vanilla essence together and add to flour mixture along with banana. Mix lightly. Spoon into greased hollows of a muffin pan until two-thirds full. Bake at 200 °C for 20 minutes. Turn out onto a cooling rack.

Makes 24 muffins

# Health muffins

A wholesome treat for the lunch box. A cream cheese topping will transform one of these muffins into a delicious mouthful of carrot cake!

   140 g self-raising flour (250 ml)
   3 ml bicarbonate of soda
   2 ml salt

*Thyme and tomato muffins (p. 61)*

   5 ml ground cinnamon
   2,5 ml mixed spice
   60 g whole-wheat flour (125 ml)
   grated rind of 1 lemon
   250 ml grated carrots
   125 ml tinned crushed pineapple, drained
   75 ml each seedless raisins and coarsely chopped
      pecan nuts
   2 eggs, beaten
   150 ml cooking oil
   100 g brown sugar (125 ml)
   12 whole walnuts

Sift self-raising flour, bicarbonate of soda, salt, cinnamon and mixed spice together. Add whole-wheat flour, lemon rind, carrots, pineapple, raisins and nuts, blending well. Beat eggs, oil and brown sugar together. Add to flour mixture, mixing lightly. Spoon into greased hollows of a muffin pan until two-thirds full. Top the batter in each hollow with a whole walnut. Bake at 200 °C for 20 minutes. Turn out onto a cooling rack.

Makes 12 muffins

---

VARIATION
* Omit the whole walnuts and replace with a cream cheese topping (see below).

---

# Cream cheese topping

   30 g cream cheese (30 ml)
   30 ml butter
   100 g icing sugar, sifted (180 ml)
   5 ml lemon juice
   chopped walnuts or sprinkle nuts for sprinkling

Mix cream cheese and butter until smooth. Add icing sugar and lemon juice, blending well. Spread over muffins. Sprinkle chopped walnuts or sprinkle nuts over each muffin.

# Carrot and date muffins

Dates are delicious in baked goods and also a healthy snack. Pack round, whole dessert dates into your lunch box, or cut a slab of pressed dates into bite-sized pieces.

>  120 g cake flour (250 ml)
>  15 ml baking powder
>  3 ml salt
>  50 g digestive bran (250 ml)
>  100 g sugar (125 ml)
>  65 g butter
>  50 g grated carrots (125 ml)
>  75 g finely chopped dates (125 ml)
>  2 eggs, beaten
>  165 ml milk

Sift flour, baking powder and salt together. Add bran and sugar. Rub in butter until mixture resembles crumbs. Add carrots and dates, mixing lightly. Beat eggs and milk together and add to bran mixture. Blend lightly. Spoon into greased hollows of a muffin pan until two-thirds full. Bake at 200 °C for 20 minutes. Turn out onto a cooling rack immediately.

Makes 10-12 muffins

# Baby marrow and carrot muffins

A clever way of disguising vegetables if your kids don't like them!

>  290 g self-raising flour (550 ml)
>  3 ml bicarbonate of soda
>  2 ml salt
>  5 ml ground cinnamon
>  5 ml mixed spice
>  120 g soft brown sugar (150 ml)
>  250 ml each grated carrots and baby marrows
>  50 g chopped walnuts (125 ml)
>  2 eggs, beaten

>  100 ml melted butter
>  300 ml milk

Sift self-raising flour, bicarbonate of soda, salt, cinnamon and mixed spice together. Add brown sugar, carrots, baby marrows and nuts, blending well. Beat eggs, butter and milk together. Add to mixture, blending lightly. Spoon into greased hollows of a muffin pan until two-thirds full. Bake at 200 °C for 20-25 minutes. Allow muffins to cool slightly. Turn out onto a cooling rack.

Makes 12 muffins

# Apple and cheese muffins

For a cheesier taste use 300 ml grated cheese and 200 ml grated apple. Of course, you can do it the other way round if you want these muffins to have a stronger apple flavour.

>  280 g self-raising flour (500 ml)
>  3 ml salt
>  50 ml sugar
>  100 g Tusser's cheese, grated (250 ml)
>  250 ml grated apples
>  2 eggs, beaten
>  150 ml milk
>  100 ml cooking oil
>  paprika or cayenne pepper for sprinkling

Sift self-raising flour and salt together. Add sugar, cheese and apple, mixing well. Beat eggs, milk and oil together. Add to flour mixture, blending lightly. Spoon into greased hollows of a muffin pan until two-thirds full. Sprinkle paprika or cayenne pepper on top. Bake at 200 °C for 20-25 minutes. Turn out onto a cooling rack immediately.

Makes 12 muffins

---

VARIATION
* Use Cheddar or sweet-milk cheese instead of Tusser's cheese.

# Cheese muffins

Bake the muffins in the morning, ready to be taken to work or school. If you're making large muffins, the quantity of batter will fit perfectly into a muffin pan with 6 hollows. Cheddar or Gruyère cheese may be substituted.

140 g self-raising flour (250 ml)
2 ml salt
pinch cayenne pepper
100 g grated Tusser's cheese (250 ml)
1 egg, beaten
milk
5 ml prepared mustard
grated cheese for sprinkling (optional)

Sift self-raising flour, salt and cayenne pepper together. Stir in cheese. Pour beaten egg into a measuring cup and add milk to make up 250 ml. Add to dry ingredients and blend lightly. Spoon into 10 greased hollows of a muffin pan until two-thirds full. Sprinkle cheese over, if preferred. Bake at 200 °C for 15 minutes. Turn out onto a cooling rack immediately.

Makes 10 muffins

---

VARIATION
* **Tomato and cheese muffins:** Add half a packet tomato soup powder to the dry ingredients. Sprinkle a little soup powder over each muffin before baking.

---

# Cheese and onion muffins

Read the hint on p. 24 to avoid shedding tears while preparing these deliciously moist muffins.

4 medium onions, chopped
30 ml cooking oil
3 ml dried or 10 ml chopped fresh thyme
360 g cake flour (750 ml)

10 ml baking powder
2 ml bicarbonate of soda
3 ml salt
30 ml sugar
100 g grated Gruyère or Cheddar cheese (250 ml)
2 eggs, beaten
250 ml milk
125 ml cooking oil

Sauté onions in oil. Add thyme. Sift together flour, baking powder, bicarbonate of soda and salt. Mix in sugar and cheese. Beat together eggs, milk and oil and add to flour mixture along with onion mixture. Blend lightly. Spoon into greased hollows of a muffin pan until two-thirds full. Bake at 200 °C for 20-25 minutes. Allow to cool slightly, then turn out onto a cooling rack.

Makes 15 muffins

# Thyme and tomato muffins

Spread the muffins with butter and cheese spread or fill with grated cheese.

280 g self-raising flour (500 ml)
3 ml salt
15 ml sugar
5 ml dried or 15 ml chopped fresh thyme
2 eggs, beaten
125 ml melted butter
125 ml milk
20 ml tomato paste
62,5 ml chopped peeled tomato

Sift flour and salt together. Add sugar and thyme, mixing well. Beat together eggs, butter, milk and tomato paste. Add tomato. Add egg mixture to dry ingredients, blending lightly. Spoon into greased hollows of a muffin pan until two-thirds full. Bake at 200 °C for 20-25 minutes. Turn out onto a cooling rack immediately.

Makes 10 muffins

## Bully beef muffins

These bully beef muffins are either a light meal or a giant snack in your lunch box! Use leftover topping as a Snackwich filling.

140 g self-raising flour (250 ml)
2 ml salt
1 egg, beaten
75 ml cooking oil
125 ml milk

TOPPING
2 hard-boiled eggs, shelled and chopped
1 egg, beaten
190 g tin bully beef, cubed and flaked
100 g grated Cheddar cheese (250 ml)
1 onion, chopped and fried
30 ml chutney
freshly ground black pepper to taste

Sift flour and salt together. Beat together egg, oil and milk. Add to flour mixture and blend lightly. Spoon into 11 greased hollows of a muffin pan. Combine topping ingredients and spoon onto batter in hollows. Press lightly into the batter. Bake at 200 °C for 15-20 minutes. Allow to cool slightly, then turn out onto a cooling rack.

Makes 11 muffins

## Muffins with a mince filling

Prepare a savoury mince mixture and store it in small containers as a filling for muffins, pancakes, omelettes or even tomatoes and sweet peppers.

280 g self-raising flour (500 ml)
2 ml salt
2 ml seasoning salt
1 egg, beaten
250 ml milk

100 ml melted butter
300 ml savoury mince with tomato (p. 42)
50 g Cheddar cheese, grated (125 ml)

Sift together self-raising flour, salt and seasoning salt. Beat together egg, milk and melted butter and add to dry ingredients. Blend lightly. Half-fill greased hollows of a muffin pan. Top with a little savoury mince, followed by the remaining batter. Sprinkle a little grated cheese on top. Bake at 200 °C for 20-25 minutes. Turn out onto a cooling rack immediately.

Makes 12 muffins

## Savoury muffins with ham

Spread with a flavoured butter, these muffins will be the most popular items in a picnic basket!

280 g self-raising flour (500 ml)
pinch cayenne pepper
2 ml salt
200 g ham, coarsely chopped
50 g Cheddar cheese, grated (125 ml)
5 ml dried or 15 ml fresh mixed herbs
2 baby marrows, grated
3 eggs, beaten
200 ml milk

Sift together self-raising flour, pepper and salt. Add ham, cheese, herbs and baby marrows. Beat eggs and milk together and add to mixture. Blend lightly. Spoon into greased hollows of a muffin pan until two-thirds full. Bake at 200 °C for 20-25 minutes. Turn out onto a cooling rack and leave to cool.

Makes 12 muffins

HINTS
* Use salami instead of ham.
* If self-raising flour is not available, sift together 240 g cake flour (500 ml) and 10 ml baking powder.

# Mock honey muffins

Pack these muffins in an airtight container to keep them deliciously moist. Take an extra serviette along for wiping your hands.

240 g cake flour (500 ml)
15 ml baking powder
1 ml salt
125 g hard butter
1 egg, beaten
187,5 ml milk
60 ml melted butter
125 ml honey
50 g chopped walnuts (125 ml)
5 ml ground cinnamon

Sift together flour, baking powder and salt. Grate butter into flour mixture, then rub in lightly with fingertips until mixture resembles crumbs. Beat egg and milk together and stir into flour mixture to make a soft dough. Knead lightly, then roll out into a rectangle. Brush with half the melted butter, spread half the honey over and sprinkle with walnuts and cinnamon. Roll dough up lengthwise – as you would a Swiss roll – and cut into slices of about 3 cm thick. Place slices in greased hollows of a muffin pan. Mix remaining honey and melted butter. Brush dough with this mixture, but reserve a little for later. Bake at 200 °C for 15 minutes until golden brown. Brush muffins with reserved honey and butter mixture as soon as they come out of the oven.

Makes 12 mock muffins

## Let the kids bake muffins

Muffins are the ideal lunch box snack: wholesome, filling, delicious and extremely popular with school-going children into the bargain. If there's a basic muffin mix in the refrigerator your children can bake their own muffins for taking to school. Older children can use the oven, and the younger ones the microwave (see p. 55). Additional ingredients, for example grated apple or shredded dried fruit, can be added to such a basic mix to suit everyone's taste.

## Muffins in the microwave

Sprinkle digestive bran in the greased hollows of a microwave muffin pan to ensure an attractive brown colour. Place a circle of paper towelling in the bottom of each hollow to absorb the moisture and prevent a heavy texture. To ensure that the muffins retain their shape during the baking process and to avoid, at the same time, a soggy and heavy texture, place a paper cup in each hollow of the muffin pan.

# Salad treats

## Biltong salad with lemon and fennel dressing

This salad will be popular with those fortunate enough to have a plentiful supply of this uniquely South African delicacy.

250 g moist beef biltong, thinly sliced (about 500 ml)
French salad dressing (p. 66) or 50 ml olive oil and 50 ml lemon juice
12 young spinach or other young salad leaves
125 ml bean sprouts
1 red sweet pepper, cut into julienne strips
2 hard-boiled eggs, quartered
250 ml plain or garlic croutons

LEMON AND FENNEL DRESSING
150 ml mayonnaise
150 ml sour cream
5 ml chopped fresh fennel leaves
1 small onion, grated
5 ml dried or 15 ml chopped fresh parsley
15 ml lemon juice
1 ml prepared mustard
salt and freshly ground black pepper to taste

Marinate biltong in French salad dressing or olive oil and lemon juice mixture for 4-6 hours. Lightly toss leaves and sprouts. Drain biltong and add to leaf mixture along with remaining salad ingredients, except croutons. Toss lightly. Spoon into 4 containers with lids.

*Biltong salad with lemon and fennel dressing*

Mix ingredients for lemon and fennel dressing. Pour into screw-topped jars to pack separately. Put croutons – to be scattered over each serving – in small plastic bags.

Makes 5-6 servings

---

VARIATION
* Omit the croutons, spoon salad into home-made pita breads (p. 49) and pack salad dressing separately.

---

### How to make bean sprouts

Wash the seeds (lentils, mustard seeds, sunflower seeds, mung beans or alfalfa). Remove broken seeds as well as impurities. Place about 30-45 ml in a clean jar. Cut a piece of cheesecloth to cover and over-hang the mouth of the jar. Secure the cheesecloth with a piece of string or an elastic band. Fill the jar with water and leave overnight in a warm, dark, sheltered place. Next morning, drain the seeds and rinse them through the cheesecloth. Rinse with water about 2-3 times a day and drain well. Remove the sprouts from the jar when they are about 4 cm in length and place them in indirect sunlight until they develop a green colour (chlorophyll). Store in an airtight container in the refrigerator for up to a week. Bean sprouts are very wholesome and can be enjoyed together with other ingredients in sandwiches and salads, or on their own with yoghurt.

### Hints for making salad

* Do not cut ingredients too finely, otherwise the salad will be mushy.
* Break leafy vegetables into pieces instead of cutting them.
* Toss salad ingredients lightly to avoid bruising them.
* Use salad dressing sparingly to prevent the salad becoming soggy.
* Crisp salad ingredients by rinsing them in a bowl of cold water to which 15 ml Milton or 5 ml lemon juice has been added. Pat dry with paper towelling or a clean cloth, or use a salad spinner and store in a salad crisper until needed. A plastic bag also works well.
* Pour salad dressing over just before serving, except if the salad is meant to be stored for a while. Use very little salad dressing to prevent the salad being too moist and soggy.

### SALAD DRESSINGS

* **French dressing:** In a screw-topped jar, mix 30 ml wine vinegar or lemon juice or a mixture of both, 60 ml olive oil or sunflower oil or a mixture of both, salt and freshly ground black pepper to taste, 5 ml dry mustard, pinch sugar and 5 ml dried or 15 ml chopped fresh parsley.
* **Herbed dressing:** Add 10 ml dried or 30 ml chopped fresh mixed herbs (dill, basil, parsley, sage, marjoram or chives) to French dressing. However, don't use basil and dill together. Delicious with asparagus, meat, pasta and tossed lettuce salads.
* **Garlic dressing:** Add 2 crushed cloves garlic to French dressing (see above). Delicious with cold blanched vegetables, tossed salads with leafy vegetables, or poultry.
* **Caper dressing:** Add 30 ml chopped capers to French dressing (see above). Delicious with fish salads, especially smoked fish, and chicken or smoked chicken and pasta salads.

# Stuffed tomato salad

Replace the "lids" on the stuffed tomatoes, wrap them in aluminium foil or clingwrap and pack in a lunch box.

4-6 firm, small to medium tomatoes
125 ml cold cooked rice
5 ml dried or 15 ml chopped fresh parsley
1 clove garlic, crushed
½ small onion, finely chopped or grated
30 ml French salad dressing
1 ml paprika
salt and freshly ground black pepper to taste
70 g salami, diced

Cut off the top parts ("lids") from the tomatoes, carefully scoop out the pulp and place them upside down on a plate to drain. Combine remaining ingredients and moisten mixture with 15 ml tomato pulp. Carefully spoon mixture into hollowed-out tomatoes, chill well and replace lids.

Makes 4 servings

---

VARIATION
* Substitute cold ham or tongue for the salami.

---

HINTS
* Firm medium or smallish tomatoes are easier to handle.
* 140 g uncooked rice (175 ml) yields about 500 ml cooked rice.

# Potato salad with blue cheese

When making potato salad, boil the potatoes in their jackets to prevent their absorbing too much water. If you're not very fond of blue cheese, use the smaller quantity.

12-14 new or 8 medium potatoes
4-6 rashers rindless bacon, chopped and fried until crisp

1 small onion or ½ medium onion, chopped
100 ml sour cream
200 ml mayonnaise
50-100 g blue cheese, crumbled
salt and freshly ground black pepper to taste
10 ml dried or 30 ml chopped fresh parsley

Boil potatoes in salted water until done (see hint). Skin the potatoes. Leave new potatoes whole and cube medium ones. Add remaining ingredients, tossing lightly.

Makes 6 servings

VARIATION
* Use 4-6 chopped garlic chives instead of the onion.

HINT
* Scrub the potatoes well and cook them in boiling salted water, 25 mm deep, for about 20 minutes.

# Potato salad with apple and bacon

Prepare the salad the night before, but only add the apples the next morning while filling your lunch box.

1 kg potatoes
100 g rindless bacon, coarsely chopped
5 chives, finely chopped
30 ml capers (optional)
15 ml dried or 50 ml chopped fresh parsley
salt and freshly ground black pepper to taste
200 ml mayonnaise
100 ml sour cream
2 green apples
30 ml lemon juice

Cook potatoes in their jackets until tender. Skin and cube potatoes. Fry bacon until crisp and add potatoes.

Add remaining ingredients, except apples and lemon juice, and toss lightly. Slice apples thinly, sprinkle with lemon juice and fold into potato mixture carefully.

Makes 10 servings

## Marinated potato salad

Layer 6-8 peeled, cooked and sliced potatoes, 1 chopped onion, and 1 large crushed clove garlic in a dish together with 100 g grated Cheddar cheese (250 ml). Over each potato layer, sprinkle a little salt, pepper and caraway seeds (use 5 ml in all – it may also be replaced with whole cumin). Mix 75 ml olive oil and 75 ml grape vinegar and pour over salad. Sprinkle with 30 ml chopped fresh parsley, cover and leave to stand for a few hours or overnight to allow flavours to blend. Invert dish a few times to allow oil and vinegar to permeate the salad. Makes 4-6 servings.

# Curried pasta and chicken salad with mango

Chicken, mango and curry combine to make a delicious salad that can be refrigerated in its dressing.

- 500 g rice noodles
- 4 chicken breast fillets, grilled
- 1 medium onion, chopped
- ½ cucumber, cubed
- 2 stalks celery, chopped
- 75 g seedless raisins (125 ml)
- 1 x 425 g tin mangoes, drained and cubed, or 2 medium mangoes, cubed
- 10 ml dried or 30 ml chopped fresh parsley

CURRIED MAYONNAISE
- 200 ml mayonnaise
- 30 ml lemon juice
- 75 ml chutney
- 12,5 ml mild curry powder
- salt and freshly ground black pepper to taste

First mix ingredients for curried mayonnaise and set aside. Cook rice noodles according to instructions on packet. Allow to cool. Slice chicken breasts, place in a mixing bowl and add curried mayonnaise. Add onion, cucumber, celery, raisins, mangoes and parsley to chicken and mayonnaise mixture. Add cooled rice noodles and toss lightly.

Makes 6 servings

*Curried pasta and chicken salad with mango and fruit salad*

# Fruit salad

Ideal for hot summer's days when you need something cool and refreshing. Any fruit in season may be used.

- 2 pears, peeled and cubed or sliced
- 2 apples, peeled and cubed or sliced
- 2-3 bananas, sliced
- 2 small bunches of grapes, each grape halved
- 1 papino or ½ spanspek, cubed
- 2 oranges, peeled and segmented
- a few mint leaves, chopped (optional)
- castor sugar to taste (optional)

Lightly mix fruit, mint leaves and castor sugar. Spoon into individual containers with lids and refrigerate.

Makes 6 servings

**TO TAKE ALONG:** Pack together with 175 ml strawberry yoghurt, or flavour of your choice.

VARIATIONS
* **Subtropical salad:** ½ pawpaw, scooped into balls or cubed, 2 mangoes, sliced, 3 bananas, sliced, and ¼ spanspek, scooped into balls or cubed. Sprinkle with orange juice, if preferred.
* **Granadilla sauce:** Replace the castor sugar and yoghurt with the pulp of 6 granadillas, 30 ml lemon juice and 60 ml honey. Simmer for 5 minutes, then add 25 ml rum. Chill. Add to fruit salad, stirring through lightly.
* **Dried-fruit salad:** Soak 500 g dried fruit overnight in 250 ml orange juice. Drain. Stir in 125 ml granadilla yoghurt, then spoon into containers. Take along toasted chopped nuts to sprinkle on top. Makes 4-6 servings.

# Meat and fruit salad

This salad offers the ideal way of using up leftover braaied meat, chicken, turkey or leg of lamb.

500 g cooked leftover meat, cut into thin strips
125 ml French salad dressing
2 apples, cored and thinly sliced
1 head lettuce, washed and divided into leaves

Place meat in a glass or ceramic bowl and sprinkle with salad dressing. Marinate in refrigerator for 2-3 hours. Add apple slices, ensuring that they are coated with dressing. Drain. Arrange drained meat, apple slices and lettuce in small bowls and pour remaining dressing into separate containers.

Makes 6 servings

---

VARIATION
* **Mustard and yoghurt dressing:** Replace the French dressing with the following: Mix 150 ml plain yoghurt, 15 ml grated lemon rind, 30 ml honey, 15 ml prepared mustard, salt and freshly ground black pepper to taste.

---

# Dressing for cold-meat salad

15 ml chopped fresh ginger root
150 ml orange juice
2 ml soy sauce
30 ml honey
15 ml Dijon mustard
5 ml mustard seeds

Mix ingredients together and simmer for 10 minutes, stirring continuously. Allow to cool.

# Pork and kiwi fruit salad

Kiwi fruit is available from June to November, but may be replaced with peaches, apples, grapes or bananas. If possible, keep the salad in a cool place until lunch time.

1 kg cold cooked pork, cut into paper-thin slices or strips
50 ml French salad dressing
6 kiwi fruits, thinly sliced
50 ml toasted almonds
50 ml fresh bean sprouts

CURRIED YOGHURT DRESSING
1 small onion, chopped
10 ml cooking oil
15 ml mild curry powder
100 ml mayonnaise
100 ml plain yoghurt
15 ml lemon juice
30 ml smooth apricot jam
salt and freshly ground black pepper to taste

Place meat in a container, sprinkle with French salad dressing and marinate for a few hours. Prepare curried yoghurt dressing: Sauté onion in oil until translucent. Add curry powder and fry lightly. Combine with remaining dressing ingredients, then liquidise the mixture if possible, or mix thoroughly. Place meat and kiwi fruit in individual containers. Scatter almonds and bean sprouts on top and chill well. Pour curried yoghurt dressing into small containers and pack separately, if preferred.

Makes 6-8 servings

---

VARIATION
* Spoon salad into home-made pita breads (p. 49) and pack dressing separately.

---

# Marinated vegetable salad

Vary the vegetable quantities according to taste, provided that the total weight is 1 kg.

    250 g broccoli, divided into florets
    250 g whole young green beans
    250 g baby marrows, sliced
    250 g cauliflower, divided into florets
    chicken stock or salted water for cooking
    1 large onion, chopped or sliced
    1 large red sweet pepper, seeded and chopped
    1 x 250 ml bottle French salad dressing or home-made
        French dressing (p. 66)

Cook broccoli, green beans, baby marrows and cauliflower in boiling stock or salted water for a few minutes – the vegetables should still be firm and crisp. Drain and transfer to a dish with a lid. Top with onion and sweet pepper. Pour salad dressing over hot vegetables. Cover and marinate for 4-6 hours. Using a slotted spoon, transfer to individual takeaway containers.

Makes 8 servings

---

VARIATION
* Add one or more of the following, if preferred: 100-150 g
  feta cheese cubes, 1 x 225 g tin black olives, drained, and
  12 cherry tomatoes, halved. Stir through before dishing
  out vegetables with a slotted spoon.

---

HINT
* Use 1 chicken stock cube for 500 ml boiling water.

# Cheese and mushroom salad

This salad was created from necessity, as all its ingredients are usually to be found in the grocery cupboard. It is the ideal takeaway salad, because it has to stand for a while to allow all the flavours to blend.

    300 g button mushrooms or 1 x 410 g tin mushrooms,
        drained
    200 g Cheddar cheese, cubed
    1 onion, finely chopped
    3 hard-boiled eggs, quartered
    grilled pieces of bacon for sprinkling (optional)

    DRESSING
    125 ml sour cream or plain yoghurt
    62,5 ml mayonnaise
    2 cloves garlic, crushed
    salt and cayenne pepper to taste

Steam fresh mushrooms for a few minutes. Lightly toss mushrooms, cheese, onion and eggs. Mix dressing ingredients and add to salad. Toss lightly. Spoon into containers and sprinkle bacon pieces on top.

Makes 4 servings

---

VARIATION
* Drained asparagus salad cuts may also be added.

---

# Pawpaw and avocado salad

The unusual combination of pawpaw and vegetables makes for a surprisingly delicious salad.

100 g mushrooms, sliced
1 packet mixed salad leaves
2 avocados, sliced
1 medium pawpaw or 2 small papinos, sliced or
   scooped into balls
2 stalks celery, sliced, ½ cucumber, cut into strips, or ½
   sweet pepper, seeded and cubed
2 small onions, sliced
10 ml dried or 30 ml chopped fresh parsley

DRESSING
75 ml olive oil
10 ml prepared mustard
50 ml white wine vinegar
5 ml lemon juice
30 ml honey
15 ml poppy seeds
salt and freshly ground black pepper to taste

First prepare salad dressing: Liquidise ingredients together, or mix well. Marinate mushrooms in dressing for 1-2 hours. Drain mushrooms and toss lightly with remaining salad ingredients. Pack dressing separately.

Makes 4-6 servings

HINTS
* Avocados will ripen faster if placed in a fruit bowl or basket with other fruit, or in a paper bag with a potato or an apple.
* To retard the ripening process, refrigerate the avocados until needed.
* Prevent discoloration of sauces, salsas or chilled soups containing avocado by covering them with clingwrap. Remove the air by pressing the clingwrap lightly onto the surface.
* Sprinkle lemon juice over the exposed surfaces of avocados to prevent browning.
* Storing avocados with their stones intact will also retard browning.
* Use mashed avocado in sandwiches instead of butter.

* Mashed avocado sprinkled with lemon juice can be frozen in freezer bags. Use it in dishes where appearance is of secondary importance, e.g. in a chilled pancake filling.

## Crudités

CRUDITÉS (raw vegetable sticks and pieces) are the ideal takeaway meal for health-conscious people. Rather select 2 or 3 kinds of vegetables that are crisp and fresh than a wider variety of poor quality. Pack a dip to take along.

BABY MEALIES  Leave whole or halve lengthwise.
BROCCOLI AND CAULIFLOWER  Divide into small florets.
CARROTS  Scrape and cut into julienne strips.
GREEN AND RED SWEET PEPPERS  Seed and cut into julienne strips.
FRESH YOUNG GREEN BEANS  Top and tail.
BUTTON MUSHROOMS  Wipe clean with paper towelling and halve, if necessary.
CUCUMBERS  Cut into thick strips (remove seeds, if preferred).
MANGETOUT (SUGAR PEAS)  Top and tail only.
BABY MARROWS  Cut off ends and cut lengthwise into 4 strips or sticks.
CELERY  Cut into sticks 8-10 cm in length.
CHERRY TOMATOES  Simply wipe clean and leave whole.
SPRING ONIONS  Neatly trim tops and cut off roots.

Pack together with an onion, curry-flavoured, tomato, seafood or avocado dip (see pp. 17-18).

# Roulade with tuna salad filling

This may sound a trifle exotic, but don't be afraid to tackle the recipe. If you can make a white sauce, this soufflé roll will be child's play.

ROULADE
1 small onion, grated
1 clove garlic, crushed
70 g butter (75 ml)
60 g cake flour (125 ml)
1 ml salt
500 ml milk
4 eggs, separated

TUNA SALAD FILLING
1 x 200 g tin tuna, drained
1 avocado, peeled and cubed
5 ml lemon juice
60 ml mayonnaise
3 gherkins, finely chopped
salt and freshly ground black pepper to taste
50 g grated Cheddar cheese (125 ml)

Sauté onion and garlic in heated butter. Add flour and salt and stir-fry for 1 minute. Gradually add hot milk, stirring until sauce is smooth and thick. Allow to cool. Beat egg yolks lightly and mix in a little white sauce. Add remaining white sauce and mix well. Whisk egg whites until soft peaks form. Using a metal spoon, fold egg whites into mixture. Pour mixture into a 300 mm x 200 mm Swiss roll pan that has been greased and lined with waxed paper. Bake at 180 °C for 30-35 minutes. Allow roulade to cool, then turn out onto a wire rack covered with a clean, slightly damp kitchen towel. Carefully remove waxed paper. Cool slightly. Prepare tuna salad filling: Mix ingredients and spread over roulade. Using the kitchen towel, roll up roulade as you would a Swiss roll. Place on a serving platter, slice with a knife and egg lifter and take along as a cold meal.

Makes 6 servings

> VARIATION
> * Replace the tuna salad filling with an asparagus filling (p. 43).

# Fish finger salad

The salad dressing may be packed separately, if preferred. If possible, keep the salad in a cool place until lunch time.

15 grilled fish fingers
½ head lettuce, leaves separated and torn into pieces
1 onion, sliced
6 gherkins, halved lengthwise
2 tomatoes, sliced
1 green sweet pepper, seeded and cut into strips

SEAFOOD SALAD DRESSING
30 ml tomato sauce
pinch each cayenne pepper, paprika and salt
Tabasco sauce to taste
150 ml mayonnaise
15 ml lemon juice
30 ml vinegar
1 x 155 g tin Nestlé cream (or 150 ml cream)

Allow fish fingers to cool, then cut each into thirds. Lightly toss remaining salad ingredients, then divide among 4-6 plastic containers with lids. Prepare salad dressing: Mix tomato sauce and seasonings, then whisk in mayonnaise, lemon juice and vinegar. Add cream, whisking until mixture is smooth and creamy.

Makes 6 servings

> VARIATION
> * Add half an avocado, cut into pieces and sprinkled with lemon juice.

> ## How to cook fish fingers
>
> * Use one of four methods:
> - Bake in a preheated oven at 220 °C for 20 minutes.
> - Shallow-fry for 4 minutes on each side.
> - Deep-fry for 4 minutes in oil.
> - Brush with oil and grill for 5 minutes on each side.

# Skewered delights

## Concertina steak strips

Use leftover steak, or grill a steak, cut it into strips and thread them onto cocktail sticks to create a concertina effect.

    1 rump steak, 25 mm thick
    flavoured butter (p. 18) (optional)
    3 ml salt
    freshly ground black pepper to taste
    20 long thin wooden skewers or more cocktail sticks

Score the fatty edges at 25 mm intervals to prevent the meat from curling up while cooking. Heat a griddle pan until smoking hot. Fry meat for 5-7 minutes on each side (rare) or 7-10 minutes on each side (medium done). Remove meat from griddle pan, top with a slice of flavoured butter and leave for at least 10 minutes. Cut into thin strips. Season with salt and pepper and thread onto wooden skewers or cocktail sticks to create a concertina effect.

Makes 20 kebabs

**TO TAKE ALONG:** Dip (p. 17).

---

VARIATIONS
* **Pepper steak strips:** Season the meat strips with 10 ml coarsely ground dried green peppercorns.
* Grill the steak under a preheated oven grill or over the coals.

---

*Concertina steak strips and crudités (p. 72)*

HINT
* For added flavour, pull the wooden or bamboo skewers through a garlic clove.

---

## Cooking steaks: do's and don'ts

* Don't use commercial meat tenderisers for steak – they tend to make the meat mealy.
* Don't use a meat mallet or hammer, as it damages the meat fibres and causes loss of meat juices. Meat that has been well ripened need not be pounded.
* Don't sprinkle salt over a raw steak; it extracts meat juices and dries out the meat. Rather add salt when the steak is done.
* Turn the steak with meat tongs or even an egg lifter; a fork pierces the meat and causes meat juices to run out.
* Steak should be at least 20 mm thick; a thinner steak will be dry when cooked.
* Leave steak at room temperature for 20 minutes before cooking it. Steak that is chilled or frozen when cooked will be dry due to loss of meat juices.
* Steak should be rare or medium done to ensure maximum tenderness and juiciness.

# Smoked beef rolls with banana

8 slices smoked beef
8 cocktail sticks

FILLING
2 bananas, coarsely chopped
½ apple, coarsely grated
1 ml paprika
1 ml dry mustard
freshly ground black pepper to taste
10 ml cream
5 ml medium sherry
100 ml grated Cheddar cheese

First mix ingredients for filling. Place a teaspoonful of filling on each slice of beef. Roll up beef slices and secure with cocktail sticks.

Makes 8 rolls

# Mince sausage kebabs with a yoghurt dip

These mince sausages are delicious served cold with the yoghurt dip or a dip of your choice.

500 g lean minced beef
1 onion, finely chopped
1 clove garlic, crushed
1 carrot, grated
1 egg, beaten
salt and freshly ground black pepper to taste
5 ml dried or 15 ml chopped fresh mixed herbs
15 wooden skewers

YOGHURT DIP
½ English cucumber, seeded, grated and drained well
125 ml plain yoghurt
125 ml smooth cottage cheese
7 ml dried or 25 ml chopped fresh mint
salt and white pepper to taste

First prepare dip by mixing ingredients well. Mix mince with remaining sausage ingredients. Knead lightly. Divide into 15 balls, then shape each into a sausage around one end of each skewer. Place on the rack of an oven pan and grill 100 mm below preheated oven grill until golden brown and done. Pack cold sausages together with dip.

Makes 15 sausages

VARIATIONS
* **Ham rolls:** Spread prepared mustard on ham slices, roll up with or without an asparagus spear inside and secure with cocktail sticks.
* **Ham and pineapple rolls:** Mix 1 grated pineapple slice, 50 g chopped smoked beef and 1 chopped gherkin, and use mixture as a filling on 250 g ham slices spread with mustard. Secure with cocktail sticks.

VARIATIONS
* Replace the cucumber with chopped gherkins.
* Replace the yoghurt dip with a dip of your choice, or one of the dips on pp. 17-18.

HINTS
* Soak wooden or bamboo skewers in water for about 30 minutes to prevent them from burning during the grilling process. The ends of the skewers may also be covered with aluminium foil.
* Grill the sausages over moderate coals and serve them as a starter at a braai.
* Prepare small meatballs (p. 106) and bake at 160 °C for 12-15 minutes. Allow to cool, then thread onto bamboo skewers with cherry tomatoes, pineapple wedges, cucumber slices and blanched fresh pickling onions. Pack as a snack with or without a dip.

# Vienna and cheese kebabs

Vienna sausages, cheese and fruit on a skewer – nothing but sheer fun!

4 smoked Vienna sausages, thickly sliced
100 g Cheddar cheese, cut into fairly large cubes (250 ml)
fruit,* cubed and sprinkled with lemon juice
4 lettuce leaves, folded
extra lettuce
chutney, mustard sauce or tomato sauce (p. 16)
4 wooden skewers

Thread sausages onto skewers, alternating with cheese, fruit and lettuce leaves. Place on a lettuce leaf in lunch box. Drizzle a little chutney, mustard sauce or tomato sauce over kebabs.

Makes 4 kebabs

**TO TAKE ALONG:** Pack kebabs in hot dog rolls spread with mustard butter, in a home-made pita bread (p. 49) or even a hollowed-out French bread.

# Concertina mutton sausage with a mustard basting mixture

Soak the wooden skewers in water for 30 minutes to prevent them from burning.

500 g mutton sausage
6 wooden skewers

MUSTARD AND BEER BASTING MIXTURE
100 ml beer
15 ml prepared mustard
15 ml vinegar
15 ml chutney

Mix ingredients for basting mixture. Cut sausage into 6 pieces of equal length and thread onto wooden skewers to create a concertina effect. Grill on the rack of an oven pan under preheated oven grill, basting regularly with mixture.

Makes 6 servings

---

VARIATIONS
* **Vienna and fruit kebabs:** Use 10 smoked Vienna sausages, thickly sliced, 20 fresh strawberries, 1 pineapple, peeled and cubed, and 20 dried apricots, and thread them alternately onto wooden or bamboo skewers. Makes 10 kebabs.
* **Frankfurters and dried fruit on a skewer:** Use 8 frankfurters, quartered, 16 dried apple rings, 16 stoned prunes and 16 dried apricots, and thread them alternately onto wooden skewers. Makes 4 kebabs.

---

VARIATION
* Thread thin mutton sausage in rolls or a concertina pattern onto skewers, alternating with vegetables. Use pieces 20-25 cm in length.

---

* Use apples, spanspek, bananas or strawberries.

# Sausage wheels

Cut off part of each sosatie skewer so that it will fit into the lunch box, and wrap a serviette around the end by which it is held.

1 kg thin mutton sausage
10 wooden skewers

BASTING MIXTURE
30 ml cooking oil
50 ml fruit chutney
30 ml wine vinegar

First mix ingredients for basting mixture. Cut sausage into 10 equal pieces. Roll up each piece to resemble a snake and secure with a wooden skewer. Place sausage wheels on rack of an oven pan and grill under pre-heated oven grill for about 8 minutes. Baste with basting mixture during final 2-3 minutes' cooking time.

Makes 10 kebabs

HINTS
* For extra flavour, use a fresh herb sprig as a basting brush.
* The basting mixture has a sweet ingredient and should not be used right from the beginning, as it will burn.

---

VARIATIONS
* Thread the sausage onto the skewers to create a con-certina effect.
* The sausage wheels can also be grilled over the coals. The cooking time will remain the same.

---

# Chicken wing kebabs

Peri-peri chicken wings are the ideal takeaway snacks, especially if they are skewered and easy to handle. Cut off part of the skewer so that it will fit into the lunch box.

16 chicken wings (see hint)
16 wooden skewers
salt to taste

PERI-PERI BASTING MIXTURE
125 ml cooking oil
2 cloves garlic, crushed
5 ml peri-peri
30 ml lemon juice

Prepare the basting mixture. Heat oil in a heavy-based frying pan and fry garlic lightly until golden brown. Stir in peri-peri and lemon juice. Allow to cool. Splay out wings and thread onto skewers. Grill wings under a preheated oven grill for 15 minutes, basting regularly. Season with salt.

Makes 8 kebabs

**TO TAKE ALONG:** Dip (p. 17).

HINT
* It is advisable to remove the wing tips, as they are often "hairy" and dry and scorch easily. Use them for making stock.

*Chicken wing kebabs*

# Rainbow kebabs

Pack these kebabs together with a long bread roll spread with mustard butter – an entire light meal on a skewer!

½ cooked fresh or pickled tongue
15 small cooked meatballs (p. 106)
½ pineapple, peeled and cubed
½ x 400 g jar gherkins, sliced into rounds
15 wooden skewers
50 ml chopped fresh parsley

Allow tongue to cool in cooking liquid. Cut into cubes. Thread onto wooden skewers, alternating with meatballs, pineapple and gherkins. If too dry, sprinkle with liquid in which tongue was cooked. Coat kebabs with parsley.

Makes 15 kebabs

---

### How to cook a tongue

Place the tongue in a large saucepan and add water to cover. For extra flavour, add a bouquet garni and vegetables such as carrots, onions or celery stalks. Bring to the boil, cover with lid, reduce heat and simmer for 3-4 hours or until tender. Immerse tongue in cold water immediately, then remove skin and tubes. The tongue will be tastier if cooled in the cooking liquid.

---

# FRUIT OR VEGETABLE KEBABS

A crisp and attractive accompaniment to sandwiches. This original way of serving fruit and vegetables may just persuade your children to give these foods another try. Choose a variety of vegetables to ensure colour variation and different flavours that complement one another. It's advisable to leave fruit whole if it has to stay in the lunch box for longer than half a day.

# Vegetable kebabs

cucumber, cut into thick slices or pieces
mushrooms, whole or cut into pieces
red or green sweet pepper, seeded and cut into pieces
tomatoes, whole or quartered, or whole cherry tomatoes
baby marrows, thickly sliced
fresh pickling onions, cooked for a few minutes
lettuce leaves, separately folded or rolled up

Thread all the vegetables, except the lettuce leaves, alternately onto skewers. Wrap each kebab in a lettuce leaf, and pack.

**TAKE ALONG:** Dip (p. 17) or flavoured mayonnaise (p. 17).

---

VARIATION
* Marinate vegetable pieces in French dressing overnight or for a few hours, if preferred. Drain well and thread onto skewers.

---

HINT
* Pineapple with the vegetables will add a deliciously tropical flavour. Use a fresh pineapple, cored and cubed.

# Fruit kebabs

pineapple, peeled, cored and cubed
banana, peeled and sprinkled with lemon juice
whole strawberries, hulled
whole grapes
apples, cubed and sprinkled with lemon juice
spanspek balls or cubes
watermelon balls or cubes

Thread all the kinds of fruit alternately onto bamboo skewers. Refrigerate.

VARIATION
* Thread 200 g strawberries, 1 small pineapple, peeled and cubed, 1 bunch black grapes and 1 sweet melon, peeled, seeded and cubed, alternately onto bamboo skewers. Refrigerate. Makes 10-15 kebabs.

## Dried fruit

stoned prunes
dried figs
apple rings
dried apricots
dried peaches
dried pears

Thread dried fruit onto cocktail sticks instead of placing them singly in lunch box.

## Marinated mushrooms on skewers

It's best to use large, firm white mushrooms.

500 g mushrooms, cleaned
1 x 38 g packet Italian salad dressing
10 ml dried or 30 ml chopped fresh parsley
125 ml cooking oil
125 ml vinegar
125 ml water
6 wooden skewers or cocktail sticks

Place mushrooms in a plastic container with a lid. Mix Italian salad dressing powder, parsley, oil, vinegar and water in a saucepan and bring to the boil. Pour over mushrooms, cover with lid and leave to stand for 24 hours. Drain and thread onto cocktail sticks, or use longer skewers that will accommodate more mushrooms.

Makes 6 kebabs

**TO TAKE ALONG:** Place "mushroom kebabs" in a long bread roll spread with garlic butter and lined with lettuce leaves.

HINTS
* Rinsing mushrooms in water will make them mushy. Simply wipe them with a damp cloth before using.
* Remove any remaining mushrooms from their packaging and store them on a layer of paper towelling in a container with a lid. A brown-paper bag will also do the trick.

## Summer ham kebabs

4 thin slices of ham
8 x 15 g cheese cubes
1 mango, cubed
16 black grapes, seeded
16 green grapes, seeded

Cut ham slices into wide strips. Wrap ham strips around cheese cubes. Thread ham and cheese rolls onto cocktail sticks, alternating with mango and grapes.

Makes 4 servings

# Perfect pastry

## Vegetable tartlets

These easy-to-handle tartlets are the ideal takeaway treats.

TART PASTRY
120 g cake flour (250 ml)
2 ml salt
60 g butter
1 egg yolk, beaten
45 ml cold water

FILLING
5 baby marrows, grated
1 onion, chopped
1 clove garlic, crushed
20 ml cooking oil
1 packet white onion soup powder
1 x 250 ml container sour cream or plain yoghurt
300 g broccoli, blanched (reserve 100 ml blanching liquid)
60 g Cheddar cheese, grated (150 ml)
½ x 250 g container cottage cheese
100 g feta cheese
3 eggs, beaten
freshly ground black pepper to taste

Sift cake flour and salt together. Rub in butter. Add egg yolk and water and mix to a stiff dough. Press dough into hollows of a muffin pan to line them. Refrigerate until needed. Fry baby marrows, onion and garlic in heated oil. Mix soup powder, sour cream or yoghurt and 100 ml blanching liquid and set aside for 15 minutes. Mix all the ingredients and pour into muffin pan. Bake at 190 ˚C for 20-30 minutes or until set.

Makes 12 tartlets

*Chicken curry triangles (p. 84)*

## Picnic tartlets

Microwave the filling to save time.

1 onion, chopped
1 clove garlic, crushed
1 green sweet pepper, seeded and chopped
15 ml cooking oil
500 g minced beef
1 x 44 g packet brown onion or mushroom soup powder
250 ml meat stock or dry white wine
15 ml lemon juice
1 egg, beaten
15 ml dried or 50 ml chopped fresh parsley
50 ml sour cream
freshly ground black pepper to taste
400 g ready-made puff pastry, rolled out
beaten egg for glazing

Fry onion, garlic and sweet pepper in heated oil in a heavy-based saucepan until the onion is translucent. Add mince and fry until it changes colour. Add soup powder and stir-fry for 1 minute. Add heated stock and lemon juice and simmer until thickened. Allow meat to cool slightly, then add egg. Mix well. Add parsley, sour cream and pepper. Allow mixture to cool completely. Line greased aluminium tartlet pans, 100 mm in diameter, with puff pastry. Prick bases with a fork. Spoon filling in, cover with pastry and trim edges. Brush with egg and bake at 200 ˚C for 20 minutes or until golden brown and done.

Makes 6 tartlets

HINT
* Microwave the filling as follows: Microwave meat on 100% power for 4-5 minutes, stirring frequently. Add onion, garlic and pepper and microwave for a further 2-3 minutes. Add the remaining filling ingredients and microwave on 70% power for 6-8 minutes. Continue as described.

## Preparing pastry

* Prepare pastry on a cold working surface in a cool, airy room. If a marble surface is not available, fill a baking tray with iced water and place it on the working surface to cool it quickly and easily.
* Keep the ingredients and equipment as cold as possible to prevent the shortening from melting before the pastry is baked.
* Roll out the pastry with a wooden or marble rolling pin. Wood and marble are poor conductors of heat, so the pastry will remain cold.
* Mix the pastry with your fingertips only: they are cooler than the palms of your hands, and this method also prevents overhandling of the pastry.
* Measure out the ingredients very accurately and handle the pastry lightly, but quickly and firmly.
* Bake the pastry at the prescribed oven temperature.
* Use a spatula to separate the baked pastry from the sides of the pan and allow to cool.
* All raw pastries, except chou paste, can be refrigerated for 2-3 days or rolled out and frozen for 2-3 months.
* Fillings sometimes make pastry soggy. Prevent this by brushing the base with whisked egg white or sprinkling it with dried breadcrumbs. Bake the pastry without the filling for 2-3 minutes. A second heated baking tray can also be placed underneath the baking tray or tart dish containing the pastry.

# Sausage rolls

What could be more welcome than a flavoursome home-made sausage roll in the lunch box? With this recipe you can produce sausage rolls as your grandmother made them.

400 g minced mutton
1 small onion, chopped
1 clove garlic, crushed
salt and freshly ground black pepper to taste
1 ml dried or 3 ml chopped fresh thyme
1 egg, beaten
1 x short crust pastry (see Pastry parcels, p. 90)
beaten egg for glazing

Fry meat in heated heavy-based pan until it changes colour. Add onion and garlic and sauté. Season with salt, pepper and thyme. Bind meat mixture with egg. Roll pastry out to form a rectangle, about 3 mm thick. Spoon meat mixture on top and roll up. Cut into smaller sausage rolls. Brush with beaten egg. Bake at 210 °C for about 15 minutes.

Makes 20 small rolls

# Chicken curry triangles

Easy to make, foolproof and a full meal in itself!

1 cooked chicken, cooking liquid reserved
1 onion, chopped
1 green sweet pepper, seeded and chopped
1 clove garlic, crushed
30 ml cooking oil
10 ml curry powder
1 packet chicken noodle soup powder
500 ml chicken stock (including cooking liquid)
150 g frozen peas
1 x 440 g tin pineapple chunks, drained and cut into smaller pieces
salt, freshly ground black pepper and seasoning salt to taste
30 ml chutney
1 x 1 kg packet puff pastry squares (7 squares)
beaten egg for glazing

Bone chicken, flake meat and set aside. Fry onion, sweet pepper and garlic in heated oil until translucent. Add curry powder and stir-fry. Mix chicken noodle soup and stock and add to onion mixture along with peas. Bring to the boil and simmer until slightly thickened. Add to chicken along with pineapple. Stir in seasonings and chutney. Bring to the boil, then allow filling to cool. Spoon cold filling onto one half of each puff pastry square. Brush pastry edges with water, then fold over to form triangles. Brush triangles with beaten egg. Bake at 200 °C for 30 minutes or until golden brown and puffed up.

Makes 7 triangles

---

VARIATION
* Sprinkle sesame seeds over the pasties before baking.

---

## How to cook chicken for easy flaking

Brown a chicken in cooking oil. Add an onion and garlic and sauté. Season with salt, pepper, bay leaf and 2 whole cloves. Heat 250 ml dry white wine and 125 ml chicken stock and pour over chicken. Simmer until meat is tender and comes off the bone easily.

# Cornish pasties

1 each medium carrot, potato, turnip and onion
250 g rump steak, cut into 1,5 cm x 1,5 cm cubes
2,5 ml dried or 7 ml chopped fresh mixed herbs
5 ml dried or 15 ml chopped fresh thyme
salt and freshly ground black pepper to taste
hot-water pastry or short crust pastry (see box, right, or pastry parcels, p. 90)
30 ml butter
beaten egg or milk for glazing

Scrape carrot and peel potato, turnip and onion. Dice carrot, potato and turnip and chop onion. Mix vegetables, meat and seasonings. Roll out pastry until 3 mm thick. Using a saucer, cut out 6 circles (20 cm in diameter). Spoon meat mixture into the centre of each pastry circle. Top with 5 ml butter. Brush pastry edges with

water, press them together on top of filling and seal well. Press with fingers to obtain a zigzag effect. Make a small incision at the top of each pasty through which steam can escape. Place pasties on a greased baking tray and brush with beaten egg or milk. Bake at 200 °C for 20 minutes. Reduce temperature to 150 °C and bake for a further 35 minutes.

Makes 6 pasties

HINT
* Add initials to the pasties – just for fun: Roll out leftover pastry and use to cut out initials. Moisten with water and affix to one corner of each pasty.

---

## How to prepare hot-water pastry for pasties

Melt 125 g butter in 125 ml boiling water. Sift together 280 g self-raising flour (500 ml) and 2 ml salt. Combine with the butter mixture to form a soft dough. Place in a plastic bag or clingwrap and refrigerate for at least 1 hour.

---

## Where did Cornish pasties originate?

For many years Cornish pasties were the staple food in Cornwall, and the traditional takeaway food of the local miners, fishermen and schoolchildren. The crust, therefore, had to be substantial enough to withstand being wrapped in a cloth and carried around. According to the very first recipes there was a seam at the side which could serve as a "handle". As mealtimes were often interrupted the people had to know which pasty belonged to whom. Consequently, each person's initial was affixed to one of the top corners, forcing them to start eating from the bottom. Half of the filling often consisted of meat and the other half of fruit, e.g. apples, which served as dessert.

# Lamb pies with tomato

This tomato-flavoured pastry combines beautifully with the tasty lamb filling.

    1 kg boned neck of lamb, cubed
    30 ml cooking oil
    2 onions, chopped
    1 clove garlic, crushed
    375 ml meat stock
    5 ml dried or 15 ml chopped fresh basil
    salt and freshly ground black pepper to taste
    10 ml lemon juice
    3 carrots, sliced
    1 packet cream of tomato soup, mixed with 100 ml
        water

    PASTRY
    290 g cake flour (600 ml)
    25 ml baking powder
    1 ml salt
    50 ml butter
    100 ml tomato purée, dissolved in 50 ml water
    beaten egg for glazing

Brown meat in heated oil. Add onions and garlic and sauté until onions are translucent. Add heated stock, seasonings and lemon juice. Cover and simmer for about 1¼ hours or until meat is almost tender. Add carrots and simmer until tender. Add soup and water mixture and stir over low heat until thickened. Allow to cool. Sift together flour, baking powder and salt. Rub butter into flour mixture. Add tomato purée and water mixture and mix to a stiff dough. Roll out thinly and cut out 6 circles (15 cm in diameter). Spoon cold meat mixture onto one half of circle, brush edges with beaten egg and press together. Brush pies with beaten egg and bake at 220 ˚C for 30 minutes or until golden brown.

Makes 6 pies

*Pizza with salami (variation, p. 89)*

# Savoury lamb pies

Do not be misled into thinking that these splendid meat pies are the province of cooks with experience, luck and "pastry hands" only; they are surprisingly easy to make. And if needs must, buy ready-rolled pastry.

    4 rashers rindless bacon, chopped
    15 ml cooking oil
    750 g lamb shank, sawn into 15 mm thick slices
    1 onion, chopped
    salt and freshly ground black pepper to taste
    5 ml prepared mustard
    15 ml lemon juice
    30 ml sherry
    250 ml meat stock
    10 ml dried or 30 ml chopped fresh parsley
    cream cheese pastry (see bobotie variations, p. 105)
    beaten egg for glazing

Fry bacon in heated oil until crisp. Remove with slotted spoon and set aside. Brown meat in the same saucepan. Add onion and sauté. Season with salt, pepper, mustard, lemon juice and sherry. Add heated stock and bacon and simmer until meat starts to come off bones. Remove bones, cut meat into smaller pieces and add parsley. Cool. Roll pastry out thinly. Cut out circles with a biscuit cutter 50 mm in diameter. Spoon a little filling onto one half of each pastry circle. Brush edges with beaten egg, fold over and press edges together. Brush with beaten egg. Arrange on a baking tray and bake at 200 ˚C for 35 minutes or until golden brown.

Makes 12 pies

> VARIATION
> * Replace shank with sliced neck or cubed thick rib.

# Curried mince pies

Prepare the pies without brushing them with egg and freeze them. Bake them the night before they are to go in the lunch box.

    1 thin slice white bread
    75 ml milk
    1 small onion, finely chopped
    1 clove garlic, crushed
    15 ml cooking oil
    7 ml mild curry powder
    500 g minced beef
    5 ml brown sugar
    salt and freshly ground black pepper to taste
    30 ml seedless raisins
    15 ml wine vinegar
    50 ml meat stock
    1 bay leaf
    cream cheese pastry (see bobotie variations, p. 105) or
        ready-made puff or short crust pastry
    beaten egg for glazing

Soak bread in milk and mash with a fork. Sauté onion and garlic in heated oil. Add curry powder and stir-fry for 1-2 minutes. Add mince and fry until it changes colour. Add all the ingredients, except pastry and egg, and simmer for 15 minutes. Allow to cool, then remove bay leaf. Roll pastry out thinly and cut out 24 circles with a biscuit cutter. Brush edges of circles with beaten egg and cold water. Place spoonfuls of filling in centre of pastry circles, leaving edges uncovered. Cover filling with second pastry circle and press edges together with a fork. Prick top with a fork. Brush pies with beaten egg and arrange on a baking tray. Bake at 200 °C for 20 minutes.

Makes 12 pies

---

VARIATIONS
* Fry 5 ml chopped fresh ginger root with the onion and garlic.
* A cinnamon stick or star anise will impart a piquant taste. Remove from mince mixture before filling pies.

---

# Sandwich pies

Did you know you can make pies without an oven? These are made in the Snackwich and you can even use ready-made bought pastry.

    SHORT CRUST PASTRY
    250 g cake flour (500 ml)
    1 ml salt
    10 ml baking powder
    250 ml soft butter
    2 jumbo eggs, beaten
    1 egg white

    FILLING
    1 x 300 g tin bully beef, cut into small cubes
    2 bananas, mashed
    30 ml mayonnaise
    salt and freshly ground black pepper to taste

Sift together flour, salt and baking powder. Rub in butter until mixture resembles crumbs. Add eggs and mix to a stiff dough. Place in a plastic bag and refrigerate for 30 minutes. Meanwhile, prepare filling by mixing all the ingredients. Roll out pastry until 3 mm thick and cut into ten 12 cm rectangles. Spoon filling onto half the rectangles, brush edges with lightly whisked egg white and cover with remaining rectangles. Place pies in preheated Snackwich and toast until golden brown and done.

Makes 5 pies

HINTS
* First brush the plates of the Snackwich with cooking oil before using it. Avoid margarine, as it tends to leave a sticky layer on the plates.
* If you use too much filling, or a filling that is too runny, it will run out at the sides of the pies.

# Mini pizzas with salami

If you don't have all the ingredients for the topping at hand, use your imagination and create your own from whatever is available in the grocery cupboard.

### DOUGH
3 ml active dry yeast
125 ml lukewarm milk
5 ml sugar
15 ml melted butter
2 eggs, beaten
240 g cake flour (500 ml)
5 ml salt

### TOPPING
80 g salami slices, chopped
1 green sweet pepper, seeded and cut into julienne
    strips
black olives (optional)
150 g mozzarella cheese, grated (375 ml)
origanum for sprinkling

### TOMATO BASE
1 large onion, chopped
1 clove garlic, crushed
5 ml butter
4 tomatoes, skinned and chopped
2 ml dried or 5 ml chopped fresh basil
5 ml sugar
salt and freshly ground black pepper to taste

First prepare tomato base: Fry onion and garlic in melted butter in a heavy-based saucepan until onion is translucent. Add tomatoes, basil, sugar, salt and black pepper. Cover with lid, reduce heat and simmer for 10-15 minutes or until thickened. Allow to cool slightly. Prepare dough: Mix yeast, milk and sugar in a small dish and set aside until frothy. Stir in butter and eggs. Sift flour and salt together, make a hollow in the centre and pour yeast mixture into it. Mix to a soft dough and knead until elastic. Place dough in a greased bowl and turn over a few times until greased on all sides. Allow dough to rise in a warm place for 25 minutes. Knock down and knead a few times on a floured board. Roll dough out into 6-8 circles, 5 mm thick. Place on a greased baking tray, cover and allow to rise for 15 minutes. Cover dough with prepared tomato base and topping ingredients: salami slices, sweet pepper, olives and cheese. Sprinkle with origanum. Bake at 200 °C for 15-20 minutes.

Makes 6-8 mini pizzas

---

VARIATIONS
* Replace the salami, sweet pepper and olives with prawns, mushrooms and garlic.
* Replace the salami and olives with ham and pineapple.
* Time-saving variations:
  – Use instant yeast instead of active dry yeast and stir it into the flour before adding the other ingredients.
  – Replace the tomato base with tinned tomato and onion mix, sweetened with a pinch of sugar. Tinned savoury tomato and onion mix is also suitable.
  – Make a scone dough instead of the yeast dough: Sift together 120 g cake flour (250 ml), 2 ml cream of tartar, 1 ml bicarbonate of soda and 1 ml salt. Add 1 ml dried origanum. Rub in 30 ml butter, add 75 ml milk and mix to a soft dough. Press dough into 6-8 small greased pans. Continue as described in recipe.
* Roll dough into 1 large pizza circle and follow the method as described. Slice the baked pizza into wedges.

# Ham and cheese puffs

Make these for the lunch box, picnic basket or as a late-night TV snack.

115 g butter (120 ml)
250 ml water
120 g cake flour (250 ml)
1 ml salt
4 eggs

FILLING
150 g ham, finely chopped
250 g chunky cottage cheese with chives
50 ml mayonnaise
freshly ground black pepper to taste
paprika

Mix butter and water in a saucepan and bring to the boil. Add flour and salt at the same time and stir quickly until mixture starts to separate from the sides of the saucepan and forms a smooth ball. Remove from heat and cool slightly. Add eggs one by one, beating well after each addition. Transfer mixture to a piping bag with a star nozzle and pipe 50 mm lengths, about 20 mm apart, onto a lightly greased baking tray. Bake at 220 °C for 15 minutes, reduce temperature to 180 °C and bake for a further 10-15 minutes. Prick puffs with a sharp knife and allow to cool on a wire rack. Mix all the ingredients for the filling, except paprika. Cut puffs open, wrap in waxed paper and pack filling separately. Sprinkle paprika over before serving.

Makes 12-15 puffs

HINTS
* If the puffs brown before they feel light and firm, cover them lightly with a piece of aluminium foil. To ensure that the puffs will remain crisp, prick and return them to the oven after it has been turned off. Leave the oven door slightly ajar and allow the puffs to dry out for 30 minutes.
* If puffs become moist while in storage, dry them out again in the oven at 100 °C until crisp.
* Puffs may be stored in an airtight container for 3 days.

# Pastry parcels

Small pastry parcels (wasgoedbondeltjies) are an ideal snack for the lunch box, while the larger ones can serve as a light meal. Traditionally minced pork is used as a filling for pastry parcels, but you may use minced beef instead, if you wish.

2 medium onions, chopped
2 cloves garlic, crushed
15 ml butter or cooking oil
750 g minced pork
2-3 potatoes, peeled and diced
2 tomatoes, skinned and chopped
2 ml ground ginger
1 ml ground cloves
5 ml ground coriander
30 ml wine vinegar
salt and freshly ground black pepper to taste
100 ml meat stock

SHORT CRUST PASTRY
240 g cake flour (500 ml)
2 ml salt
125 g ice-cold butter
125 ml iced water
5 ml lemon juice or brandy
cocktail sticks and whole cloves

Fry onions and garlic in heated butter or oil. Add meat, stirring with a fork to ensure a loose texture. Fry meat until it changes colour. Add potatoes, tomatoes, spices, vinegar, salt, pepper and heated stock. Cover and simmer for 15-20 minutes. If mixture is too watery, remove lid and increase heat until liquid has evaporated. Allow meat to cool. Sift flour and salt together. Cut butter into smaller pieces and rub into mixture until it resembles crumbs. Add water and lemon juice and mix to a stiff but workable dough. Knead well. Cover pastry with clingwrap or a plastic bag and refrigerate for at least 1 hour. Roll out until 3 mm thick and cut into 90 mm x 90 mm squares. Spoon a little filling into the centre of each square. Fold the four corners together and secure with a cocktail stick and a whole clove. Pour oil into a deep-fryer or saucepan to a depth of 125 mm and deep-fry pastry parcels until golden brown. Drain the parcels on paper towelling.

Makes about 20 depending on size.

VARIATION
* Fill with cold cooked bobotie or curried mince (p. 42).

HINT
* Prevent parcels from sinking to the bottom, otherwise they will burn.

# Quick croissant hot dogs

This tasty treat is neither a croissant nor a hot dog, but incorporates elements of both!

    1 x 500 g packet self-raising flour (900 ml)
    3 ml salt
    150 g grated Cheddar cheese (375 ml)
    1 x 250 g tub smooth cottage cheese
    200 ml milk
    2 eggs, beaten
    12 Vienna sausages, halved lengthwise

Sift self-raising flour and salt together. Add 100 g (250 ml) grated cheese. Mix cottage cheese, milk and eggs and add to dry ingredients. Mix to a workable dough. Divide dough into thirds and roll out lightly into circles. Cut each circle into 8 wedges. Place a Vienna sausage on the wider side and roll dough up from this side. Place on a greased baking tray. Sprinkle with remaining cheese and bake at 200 ˚C for 20 minutes.

Makes 24 hot dogs

VARIATION
* Spread each pastry wedge with a little tomato and onion mix before wrapping the Vienna sausage in it.

# Biltong and cheese straws

A delicious snack to enjoy during the afternoon coffee break or the second break at school.

    70 g biltong, grated (150 ml)
    50 g mature Cheddar cheese, grated (125 ml)
    3 chives, chopped
    pinch cayenne pepper or freshly ground black pepper
    2 x 400 g packets ready-made puff pastry, thawed
    prepared mustard
    25 ml sesame seeds

Mix biltong, cheese, chives and cayenne pepper. On a lightly floured surface, roll out one sheet of pastry until 2-3 mm thick. Spread with prepared mustard. Spoon biltong mixture onto pastry, spreading it evenly. Roll out other sheet of pastry and place on top of filling. Press together lightly. Cut pastry crosswise into 150 mm x 15 mm strips. Twist strips into spirals and arrange on a greased baking tray. Sprinkle with sesame seeds and bake at 200 ˚C for 20-25 minutes or until well puffed up and golden brown. Allow straws to cool slightly on baking tray, then transfer them to a cooling rack until cold.

Makes about 12 straws

VARIATION
* Replace the biltong mixture with 125 g crumbled blue cheese, 1 beaten egg and 5 ml dry mustard.

HINT
* The unbaked straws, lightly covered, can be refrigerated for a few hours before baking. They can also be frozen, unbaked, for up to a month. The baked straws can be kept in an airtight container for a few days.

# Snoek quiche

A quiche can be served as a starter or a light meal accompanied by a crisp salad, but is just as suitable for a lunch box or a picnic basket. Virtually foolproof, easy to prepare and utterly delicious!

PASTRY
100 g cake flour (250 ml)
50 g grated Cheddar cheese (125 ml)
125 ml butter, grated

FILLING
250 ml smoked flaked snoek
15 ml chopped capers* (optional)
4 eggs, beaten
175 ml plain yoghurt
250 ml cream
5 ml prepared mustard
salt and freshly ground black pepper to taste

Mix ingredients for pastry to a stiff dough – preferably in a food processor. Press onto base and against sides of a quiche dish (220 mm in diameter) or 6 individual quiche pans. Scatter snoek and capers over pastry. Beat together eggs, yoghurt, cream and mustard. Season with salt and pepper. Pour over snoek and bake at 180 °C for 35 minutes or until egg custard is firm and a knife-point inserted at the centre of the filling comes out clean.

Makes 1 quiche or 6 individual quiches

```
VARIATIONS
* Replace the pastry with a ready-made pastry roll.
* Replace the capers with 15 ml chopped fresh parsley to
  lend colour to the quiche.
```

* Capers are small olive-green buds (of a shrub) that are pickled and bottled. They are usually sold in small glass jars at large supermarkets. Capers impart a piquant flavour to white sauce, mayonnaise, tartar sauce and salad, and can also be used to garnish open sandwiches.

# Sausage and cheese quiche

You may even use leftover sausage for this quiche. See also the appetizing filling variations on p. 93.

WHOLE-WHEAT CRUST
140 g whole-wheat flour (250 ml)
60 ml self-raising flour
110 g ice-cold butter
125 ml plain yoghurt

FILLING
3 pork sausages or 3 pieces of boerewors
5 thin slices Cheddar cheese (about 50 mm squares)
1 tomato, skinned, quartered and sliced
4 chives or ½ onion, chopped
½ small sweet pepper, seeded and chopped
15 ml butter
10 ml dried or 30 ml chopped fresh parsley
250 ml cream or milk
175 ml plain yoghurt
3 eggs
salt and freshly ground black pepper to taste

Lightly mix whole-wheat and self-raising flour. Grate butter coarsely and rub into flour with your fingertips until mixture resembles coarse mealie meal. Stir in yoghurt and mix to a stiff dough. Cover dough and refrigerate for 30 minutes. Roll dough out thinly and use to line a quiche dish (220 mm) or 6 small quiche dishes. Prick base of pastry lining, cover and refrigerate for a further 30 minutes. Bake blind at 200 °C (see p. 93). Remove paper and beans or rice and bake for a further 5 minutes. Fry sausage in griddle pan until brown and nearly cooked. Cut into slices. Line quiche crust with cheese slices, followed by tomato slices and, lastly, sausage slices. Sauté onion and sweet pepper in heated butter and sprinkle over filling. Beat remaining ingredients together. Pour egg mixture into crust and bake at 180 °C for 45 minutes or until egg custard has set.

Makes 1 quiche or 6 individual quiches

VARIATIONS
* Use ready-made short crust pastry.
* Sauté one ingredient from each group in the heated butter and use as a filling:
- Ham, bacon, smoked beef, biltong, tuna, smoked snoek and cooked flaked chicken.
- Mushrooms, leeks, asparagus, tomato, onions, chives, olives, sweet pepper, artichoke hearts, spinach.
- Cheddar cheese, Parmesan cheese, Gruyère cheese, blue cheese, cottage cheese.
- Fresh or dried herbs.

HINTS
* Place sausages in a cold griddle pan and heat slowly to prevent the casing from splitting. Instead of a fork, use meat tongs or an egg lifter to turn the sausages.
* The cooked quiche crust can be placed in an airtight container and kept in a cool, dry place for a week, or it may even be frozen for 3-6 months. The filling is prepared and baked just before use. It is not necessary to thaw the crust. The filled crust cannot be frozen, as the liquid will separate during the thawing process.
* Do not fill a quiche crust more than three-quarters of the way, as the volume of a quiche filling increases during the baking process.
* Insert a knife-point into the centre of an egg custard filling – if it comes out clean, the filling is cooked.
* Cool a quiche slightly before cutting it.

## How to bake pastry blind

Cover pastry with waxed paper, fill with dried beans or rice and bake in a preheated oven at 200 °C for 10 minutes. Remove beans and waxed paper and bake for another 3 minutes to dry out further. To prevent the crust from absorbing too much liquid during baking, it may be brushed lightly with whisked egg white after the paper and beans have been removed, and then baked for a further 3 minutes.

## How to compile a quiche recipe

It should contain at least 3 eggs, at least 425 ml liquid (cream, milk, evaporated milk, sour cream or plain yoghurt and combinations), 250 ml of the ingredient determining its flavour, e.g. ham, asparagus or spinach, and seasonings. By varying the filling ingredients you can create numerous new combinations to suit your taste and pocket.

# To reheat and enjoy. . . .

## Baked potatoes with cottage cheese and sour cream

It is a little-known fact that potatoes are an important source of vitamin C. In addition, the best potatoes keep on their jackets for a meal and are therefore the perfect choice for your lunch box.

6 potatoes
butter (optional)
125 g smooth cottage cheese with chives
125 ml sour cream

Wash and scrub potatoes, dry and prick skins to prevent potatoes from splitting. Bake potatoes at 200 ˚C for 45-60 minutes or until tender. Remove potatoes from oven. Make two deep crosswise incisions in the centre of each potato. Gently squeeze potatoes on either side and top with a pat of butter, if preferred. Mix cottage cheese and sour cream and pack separately from potatoes, which can be wrapped in aluminium foil. Just remember to remove the foil before reheating potatoes in the microwave oven.

Makes 6 servings

*Baked patoto with cottage cheese and sour cream*

VARIATIONS
* Replace the cottage cheese and sour cream with a flavoured butter (p. 18).
* Sprinkle chopped chives over the potato.
* **Potatoes with tomato and onion filling:** Peel the potatoes and coat them with soup powder. Place each on the shiny side of a piece of aluminium foil and wrap up. Bake at 200 ˚C until done. Unfold foil and make a crosswise incision in each potato. Open the potato. Heat a tin of tomato and onion mix and place a spoonful in each potato. Sprinkle with cheese, and pack.
* A little cayenne pepper or crisply fried, chopped bacon will add interest to a potato with sour cream.
* See p. 43 for more fillings for potatoes.

HINT
* Open each potato like a flower by using your index finger and, of course, oven gloves.

## How to bake a potato

Wash and dry the potato thoroughly. You may also prick it with a testing skewer to ensure that the steam will escape and to prevent the potato from splitting. Place the uncovered potato on the oven rack. Wrapped in aluminium foil, the potato tends to steam instead of bake. If you want the skin to be soft, rub the potato with oil beforehand. For a crisper skin, rub it with salt before baking it. The potato is done if it feels soft when pressed; it can also be tested with a testing skewer. Usually a crosswise incision is made in the potato, the flesh is squeezed out slightly from the outside, and the potato is served with a filling in the open part.

# Apple cheezas

Place these cheezas under your grill at home until golden brown, and simply reheat them in that miraculous little oven at the office.

1 small onion, grated
1 green apple, grated
15 ml butter
30 ml mayonnaise
1 egg yolk, slightly beaten
125 g ripe Camembert, mashed
10 slices rye bread

Sauté onion and apple in melted butter. Combine apple mixture, mayonnaise, egg yolk and cheese. Spread mixture on rye bread and grill under preheated oven grill until slightly browned.

Makes 10 cheezas

---

VARIATION
* **Asparagus cheezas:** Replace the apple with chopped asparagus salad cuts.

---

# Bean and tomato dip

This bean and tomato dish is easy to make. It is reheated in the microwave oven and serves as a dip for potato chips.

1 large onion, chopped
1 large clove garlic, crushed
½ green sweet pepper, seeded and chopped
20 ml cooking oil
1 x 410 g tin tomato and onion mix
1 x 410 g tin speckled red kidney beans, drained
15-20 ml chilli sauce
100 g grated Cheddar cheese (250 ml)

Sauté onion, garlic and sweet pepper in oil until onion is transparent. Add tomato and onion mix and beans and season with chilli sauce. Spoon into 6 small bowls and sprinkle cheese on top.

Makes 6 servings

**TO TAKE ALONG:** A packet of Big Korn Bites for everyone.

# Pancake bake

Prepare this delicious pancake treat, but be sure to use individual china dishes (with plastic lids) that can be taken to the office.

PANCAKES
pancake batter (p. 52)

FILLING
12 thin slices of ham
12 thin slices of Gruyère or Cheddar cheese

TOPPING
175 ml plain yoghurt
250 ml sour cream
3 jumbo eggs, beaten
salt and freshly ground black pepper to taste
100 g grated Cheddar or Gruyère cheese (250 ml)

Mix pancake batter, bake 12 pancakes and set aside. Top each pancake with a slice each of ham and cheese, roll up and place in pairs in small, greased oven dishes. Whisk the topping ingredients, except the cheese, together and pour over pancakes. Sprinkle cheese over and bake at 180 °C for 15-20 minutes until set.

Makes 6 servings

# Mock cannelloni

Freeze the unbaked mock cannelloni in individual dishes, and remove from the freezer 2 hours before baking it.

PANCAKES
pancake batter (p. 52)
savoury mince with tomato (p. 42)

TASTY TOMATO SAUCE
125 g rindless bacon, chopped
1 large onion, chopped
1 clove garlic, crushed
100 ml tomato purée
200 ml chicken stock
1 ml pepper

CHEESE SAUCE
25 ml butter
25 ml cake flour
salt and pepper to taste
250 ml milk
100 g grated Cheddar cheese (250 ml)

Mix pancake batter and bake 12 pancakes. Prepare savoury mince. Make tasty tomato sauce: Fry bacon, then add onion and garlic. Add remaining ingredients and simmer for 10 minutes. To make cheese sauce, melt butter and stir in flour and seasonings. Gradually stir in heated milk. Simmer for a few minutes until thickened. Remove from heat and stir in half the cheese. To assemble: Fill pancakes with savoury mince with tomato. Layer pancakes in an oven dish or 6 small oven dishes. Spoon tasty tomato sauce over each layer of pancakes. Top with cheese sauce and sprinkle with remaining cheese. Bake at 180 °C for 30 minutes or until heated through and cheese has melted.

Makes 6 servings

HINT
* Prepared – but unbaked – mock cannelloni can be frozen in an airtight container for up to 1 month. Remove from the freezer 2 hours before serving.

# Shell noodles with tuna and tomato

A pasta dish can be prepared in a jiffy, especially if the main ingredients come from tins and packets as in this recipe.

1 onion, chopped
1 clove garlic, crushed
1 stalk celery, chopped
15 ml cooking oil
1 x 410 g tin tomato and onion mix with garlic, origanum and basil
salt and freshly ground black pepper to taste
2 ml sugar
1 x 185 g tin tuna
½ packet mushroom soup powder
125 ml milk
300 g shell noodles
75 g grated Cheddar cheese (187,5 ml)
Parmesan cheese

Fry onion, garlic and celery in oil. Add tomato and onion mix and season with salt, pepper and sugar. Add tuna and soup powder mixed with milk, and simmer until thickened. Cook pasta according to instructions on packet. Stir sauce and Cheddar cheese into pasta. Spoon into 4 suitable small bowls with lids. Pack Parmesan cheese separately.

Makes 4 servings

## How to cook pasta

Using a deep saucepan, cook 500 g pasta in 3 litres boiling water to which 10 ml salt and 5 ml cooking oil have been added. Make sure that the water is boiling rapidly before adding the pasta. Add the pasta a little at a time to prevent the water cooling off too rapidly. Stir occasionally. Cook for 7-9 minutes at sea level and 9-12 minutes in the interior until tender, but still firm. Drain through a colander, retaining about 30 ml water to prevent the pasta from drying out. Sprinkle with a little oil or stir in a knob of butter. Mix lightly but thoroughly.

# Screw noodles with ham and mushrooms

Pasta can be reheated very successfully, particularly in the microwave oven.

    300 g screw noodles
    1 onion, chopped
    2 cloves garlic, crushed
    25 ml cooking oil
    250 g fresh mushrooms, sliced
    200 g ham, diced
    1 x 47,5 g packet German Wild Mushroom Sauces of the
        World
    300 ml cold milk
    salt and freshly ground black pepper to taste
    250 ml sour cream
    5 ml dried or 15 ml chopped fresh parsley

Cook pasta according to instructions on packet. Meanwhile, fry onion and garlic in oil. Add mushrooms and ham and fry lightly. Mix mushroom sauce with cold milk, then add to contents of saucepan. Add seasonings and bring to the boil. Reduce heat and simmer for 3 minutes. Stir in sour cream and pasta and heat through, but do not allow to boil. Spoon into 4 suitable small bowls with lids and sprinkle with parsley.

Makes 4 servings

**TO TAKE ALONG:** Parmesan cheese in a small separate container, for sprinkling on top.

# Fish with mussels and asparagus

Use loin cuts, as they are smaller and more manageable. They may even be halved to facilitate eating them with a fork.

    1 x 700 g packet hake loin cuts
    1 x 105 g tin smoked mussels, drained (reserve oil)
    30 ml butter
    60 ml cake flour
    1 x 290 g tin asparagus salad cuts, drained (reserve liquid)
    250 ml milk
    salt and pepper to taste
    100 ml plain yoghurt
    15 ml lemon juice
    100 g grated Cheddar cheese (250 ml)
    cooked rice

Arrange fish in an oven dish with a lid. Drain mussels and spoon on top of fish. Heat reserved oil from mussels and butter in a saucepan. Stir in flour. Heat 100 ml asparagus liquid together with 250 ml milk and gradually add to flour mixture. Stir until thickened. Season with salt and pepper. Remove from heat and add yoghurt and lemon juice. Stir in cheese. Arrange asparagus cuts on top of fish. Pour sauce over fish, cover with lid and bake at 180 °C for 30 minutes. Remove lid and bake for a further 15 minutes. Spoon onto rice in 6 small individual dishes with lids. Refrigerate before taking it away.

Makes 6 servings

*Asparagus cheezas (variation, p. 96)*

HINT
* You may also use a larger tin of asparagus salad cuts.

# Tertia's curry stew

Ring the changes with a delicious home-cooked meal at the office, instead of the usual sandwiches.

    1 kg boned shin of beef, cut into 15-20 mm cubes
    30 ml cooking oil
    2 onions, sliced
    1 each red and green sweet pepper, seeded and cut
        into strips
    5 ml chopped fresh ginger root
    2 cloves garlic, crushed
    5 ml marsala
    5 ml turmeric
    2 ml nutmeg
    knife-point mixed spice
    2 whole cloves
    1 star anise
    2 cinnamon sticks
    5 ml brown sugar
    salt and freshly ground black pepper to taste
    350 ml meat stock
    350 g mixed dried fruit
    100 ml fruit chutney
    15 ml grated orange rind
    coconut for sprinkling

Brown meat in heated oil in a heavy-based saucepan. Remove from saucepan and set aside. Sauté onions, sweet peppers, ginger and garlic. Add spices and stir-fry. Season with sugar, salt and pepper. Add heated stock, cover with lid and simmer until meat is almost tender. Add dried fruit, chutney and orange rind, then simmer until fruit is tender. Remove cinnamon, star anise and cloves. Dish out and sprinkle with coconut.

Makes 6 servings

---

VARIATION
* Instead of turmeric, use 2-3 strands of saffron, soaked in 50 ml of the stock for 20 minutes. Add to the saucepan along with the rest of the heated stock.

---

HINT
* Tie the star anise, cinnamon sticks and cloves in a piece of muslin for easy removal afterwards.

# Savoury mince pie

A mince bake with a tasty yoghurt topping. Allow the hot dish to cool, then freeze individual portions in containers suitable for taking along to work.

    350 g minced beef
    10 ml cooking oil
    1 onion, chopped
    1 clove garlic, crushed
    1 stalk celery, chopped
    100 g mushrooms, sliced
    10 ml mild curry powder
    15 ml cake flour
    125 ml chicken stock
    30 ml tomato purée

    TOPPING
    250 ml plain yoghurt
    2 large eggs, beaten
    50 ml cake flour
    50 g Cheddar cheese, grated (125 ml)
    salt and freshly ground black pepper to taste

Fry meat in heated oil in a heavy-based saucepan until it changes colour. Add onion, garlic, celery, mushrooms and curry powder and sauté until onion is translucent. Stir in flour, heated stock and tomato purée. Simmer for 5 minutes until slightly thickened. Spoon meat mixture into an oven dish or 4 small individual oven dishes. Mix ingredients for topping. Pour yoghurt mixture over mince. Bake at 160 °C for 30 minutes or until topping is set and golden brown.

Makes 4 servings

**TO TAKE ALONG:** Salad or a few crudités (p. 72).

# All-in-one mince casserole

A flavoursome one-dish meal containing mince, vegetables and rice which can be frozen successfully in takeaway portions.

500 g minced beef
10 ml cooking oil
2 onions, chopped
1 clove garlic, crushed
1 green sweet pepper, seeded and chopped
200 g uncooked rice (250 ml)
10 ml mild curry powder
3 tomatoes, skinned and chopped
200 g fresh green beans, shredded
salt and freshly ground black pepper to taste
50 ml fruit chutney
300 ml chicken stock

Fry mince in heated oil in a heavy-based saucepan until it changes colour. Remove meat from saucepan. Sauté onions, garlic and sweet pepper in the same saucepan until onions are translucent. Add rice and curry powder and fry lightly for 2 minutes. Spoon meat on top of rice mixture, then layer tomatoes and green beans on top of meat. Heat seasonings, chutney and stock and add to contents of saucepan. Cover with lid, reduce heat and simmer for 30 minutes or until rice is tender.

Makes 6 servings

VARIATION
* Replace the fruit chutney with tomato or banana and raisin chutney (p. 16)

# Potato and cheese sausage dish

For a single person, this all-in-one sausage dish is just enough for one meal and a takeaway portion the following day.

1 large onion, chopped
100 g mushrooms, sliced
30 ml butter
100 g cheese sausage, sliced
2 medium potatoes, cooked, skinned and sliced
2 baby marrows, cooked and sliced
50 g Cheddar cheese, grated (125 ml)

MUSTARD SAUCE
25 ml sugar
10 ml dry mustard
3 ml cake flour
salt and freshly ground black pepper to taste
20 ml vinegar
60 ml water
1 egg
50 ml plain yoghurt
5 ml whole-grain or Pommery mustard

First prepare mustard sauce. Mix sugar, dry mustard, flour, salt and pepper in a small saucepan. Add vinegar and water, mixing well. Slowly bring to the boil. Beat egg and stir in a little of the hot sauce. Add egg mixture to sauce in saucepan and stir over moderate heat until thick and smooth – do not allow sauce to boil. Allow to cool, then stir in yoghurt and whole-grain mustard. Fry onion and mushrooms in butter. Heat cheese sausage in boiling water in a saucepan. Layer potato slices, onion and mushroom mixture, baby marrows and sausage in a greased oven dish or 2 smaller oven dishes, ending with a layer of sausage. Cover with mustard sauce and sprinkle Cheddar cheese on top. Place under a preheated oven grill until cheese has melted.

Makes 1-2 servings

# Rich man's chicken

Use small, manageable chicken portions such as drumsticks and thighs for this dish. Accompanied by rice it will make a memorable takeaway meal. Increase the quantity of cheese by half to make it even more special.

12 chicken drumsticks or 8 thighs
15 ml butter and 15 ml cooking oil
1 x 410 g tin asparagus salad cuts (reserve liquid)
salt and freshly ground black pepper to taste
5 ml dry mustard
1 x 410 g tin whole mushrooms, drained
50 ml cake flour
400 ml milk
100 ml plain yoghurt
30 ml lemon juice
100 g grated Cheddar cheese (250 ml)

Fry chicken in heated butter and oil. Pour off rendered fat and set aside. Add asparagus liquid to chicken, season with salt, pepper and mustard and simmer for 1 hour. Arrange chicken pieces in a casserole and top with asparagus cuts and mushrooms. Heat reserved fat and add flour, followed by cooking liquid of chicken and hot milk. Stir until thickened. Remove from heat and add yoghurt, lemon juice and half the cheese. Pour over chicken in casserole, sprinkle remaining cheese over and bake at 160 °C for 30 minutes.

Makes 4-6 servings

# Bacon and mushroom pasta dish

Nowadays many employers provide microwave ovens for heating lunches such as this tasty pasta dish.

1 x 500 g packet ribbon noodles
1 x 250 g packet rindless bacon, shredded
10 ml butter or cooking oil
2 medium onions, chopped
4 cloves garlic, crushed
250 g uncooked mushrooms, sliced
2-3 baby marrows, grated
1 packet mushroom soup powder
500 ml milk
250 ml cream
50 g grated mature Cheddar cheese (125 ml)
salt and freshly ground black pepper to taste

Cook pasta according to instructions on packet. Fry bacon in a heavy-based saucepan until crisp. Remove and set aside. Add butter or oil to rendered fat and fry onions, garlic, mushrooms and baby marrows. Return bacon to saucepan and remove from heat. Add fried ingredients to cooked noodles, blend lightly and set aside to keep warm. Return saucepan to stove and add mushroom soup powder and milk. Bring to the boil, stirring continuously. Simmer for a few minutes. Add cream, cheese and pasta, season with salt and pepper and heat through, but do not allow to boil.

Makes 6-8 servings

**TO TAKE ALONG:** Grated Parmesan cheese.

# Pastitsio

This Greek meat pie, consisting of layered macaroni and savoury mince with a creamy topping, is cut into squares and traditionally served lukewarm or cold. South Africans seem to prefer the warm version.

2 onions, chopped
1 clove garlic, crushed
10 ml cooking oil
500 g minced beef
50 ml tomato paste
salt and freshly ground black pepper to taste
1 ml ground cinnamon
5 ml dried or 15 ml chopped fresh thyme
1 ml grated nutmeg

250 g cooked macaroni, noodles or spaghetti (550 ml)
75 ml grated Parmesan cheese

CHEESE SAUCE
50 g butter
50 ml cake flour
500 ml milk
150 g Cheddar cheese, grated (375 ml)
3 ml salt
pinch cayenne pepper
250 ml plain yoghurt

Sauté onions and garlic in heated oil in a heavy-based saucepan until onions are translucent. Add meat and fry until it changes colour. Add tomato paste and seasonings. Prepare the cheese sauce: Melt butter in a heavy-based saucepan. Add flour and stir with a wooden spoon over low heat for 3 minutes. Remove from heat and gradually add milk, stirring continuously. Return to stove, bring to the boil and stir continuously until sauce is smooth. Reduce heat and simmer for 2 minutes, stirring occasionally. Remove from heat and add half the cheese and the seasonings. Stir in yoghurt. Mix macaroni with half the Parmesan cheese. Turn macaroni into an oven dish and pour half the sauce over it, followed by meat and remaining sauce. Top with remaining cheese and bake at 160 °C for about 45 minutes. Leave in warming drawer for 10 minutes. Cut into squares.

Makes 6 servings

# Moreish meat

## Bobotie for takeaways

A basic bobotie recipe can be used to prepare the most sumptuous finger foods. And don't forget the taste sensation provided by bobotie and chutney as a sandwich filling!

    1 thick slice white bread
    250 ml milk
    2 onions, chopped
    1 clove garlic, crushed
    30 ml butter
    1 kg minced beef, lamb or mutton
    30 ml mild curry powder
    15 ml turmeric
    salt and freshly ground black pepper to taste
    30 ml wine vinegar
    5 ml brown sugar or 15 ml apricot jam
    12 almonds, crushed (optional)

    TOPPING
    2 eggs
    salt and freshly ground black pepper to taste
    6 orange, lemon or bay leaves

Soak bread in 125 ml milk, then crumble. Sauté onions and garlic in heated butter in a heavy-based saucepan until translucent. Add mince and fry until it changes colour. Add curry powder and turmeric and stir-fry for 1 minute. Stir in remaining bobotie ingredients, except the remaining milk. Transfer to a greased pie dish and spread evenly. Prepare topping: Beat together eggs, remaining milk and seasonings. Pour over meat. Arrange orange, lemon or bay leaves on top and bake at 160 ˚C for 30 minutes. Remove leaves.

Makes 8 servings

VARIATIONS

* **Bobotie snacks:** Add 1-2 eggs to basic recipe. Transfer the mixture to a greased oven dish, pour topping over and bake at 160 ˚C for 30 minutes. Allow to cool. Cut into squares and spread with smooth apricot jam, tomato, banana and raisin (p. 16) or ordinary chutney. Top each square with a piece of fried banana.
* **Bobotie parcels:** Prepare cream cheese pastry (see below) or use shop-bought short crust pastry. Cut the pastry into small squares. Omit the topping. Spoon a little of the bobotie mixture onto each pastry square. Fold opposite corners of the square together and seal with water, beaten egg or milk. Secure with a cocktail stick and clove. Deep-fry until golden brown. Drain on paper towelling and allow to cool before placing in lunch box.
* **Bobotie tartlets:** Prepare miniature tartlet cases with cream cheese pastry (see below) or small pancakes (see p. 52 for pancake batter). Place the pancakes in the greased hollows of a muffin pan. Fill the tartlet cases or pancakes with basic bobotie mixture. Pour a little of the topping over and bake the filled tartlet cases at 180 ˚C for 7-10 minutes, and the pancakes for 12-15 minutes.
* **Cream cheese pastry:** Sift together 240 g cake flour (500 ml), 1 ml salt and 5 ml dry mustard. Cut 125 g ice-cold butter into smaller pieces and rub lightly into flour mixture with your fingertips. Add 1 x 250 g tub cream cheese, a spoonful at a time, to form a stiff dough. Place the dough in a plastic bag and refrigerate for 30 minutes. Roll out thinly and use.

*Spicy chicken drumsticks (p. 106)*

# Savoury meatballs

Meatballs may be frozen for up to 2 months. Thaw overnight in packaging and use for a takeaway meal.

> 1 onion, chopped
> 10 ml cooking oil
> 100 ml fresh breadcrumbs
> 100 ml milk
> salt and freshly ground black pepper to taste
> 1 ml each ground cloves and nutmeg
> 3 ml dried or 10 ml chopped fresh mixed herbs
> 25 ml each chutney and tomato sauce
> 10 ml Worcester sauce
> 500 g minced beef

Sauté onion in heated oil in a heavy-based saucepan until translucent. Soak breadcrumbs in milk. Using two forks, lightly blend all ingredients. Shape meatballs and arrange on a baking tray. Bake at 160 °C for 25-30 minutes. If preferred, place under a preheated oven grill to obtain an attractive brown colour.

Makes 6 servings

---

VARIATIONS
* Replace the breadcrumbs with grated apple or carrot, chopped dried fruit or chopped nuts.
* The meatballs may also be coated with a batter or crumbs, and shallow-fried.
* Shape meatballs around a cube of cheese.

---

# Spicy chicken drumsticks

No long journey or picnic will be complete without these special drumsticks in the food basket!

> 1 x 32 g packet French salad dressing
> 200 ml cooking oil
> 1 x 28 g packet chicken marinade
> 175 ml cold water
> 12 chicken drumsticks
> barbecue mixture for chicken*

Mix French salad dressing and cooking oil. Mix chicken marinade and water until smooth. Combine two mixtures and use to marinate chicken overnight. Grill over moderate coals or under a preheated oven grill until cooked. Season with barbecue mixture for chicken. Allow to cool and refrigerate until needed.

Makes 6-8 servings

* This exceptional barbecue mixture consists of equal quantities of the following: barbecue mix, barbecue spice and steak and chops seasoning.

---

### How to make snacks from chicken drumsticks or wings

Chop off both bone knobs from the chicken drumstick. Use a chef's knife or meat axe for this task. Using a smaller knife, press the meat and skin 1-2,5 cm up from the thin end of the bone towards the meaty end. Use the same technique to make 2 smaller snacks from a chicken wing that has been halved at the joint and of which the wing tip has been removed.

# Special chicken patties for the road

Pack into a suitable food container with a tight-fitting lid and refrigerate until departure. For a long journey it's advisable to use a cool bag.

PATTIES
750 g finely chopped cooked chicken
125 ml dried breadcrumbs, or the savoury kind
5 ml dried or 15 ml chopped fresh parsley
2 chives, chopped
salt and freshly ground black pepper to taste
pinch dried mixed herbs or 5 ml chopped fresh mixed
    herbs (e.g. sage, thyme and rosemary)
1 x 170 g tin evaporated milk

FILLING
250 g rindless bacon, shredded
1 onion, peeled and chopped
15 ml chutney
15 ml tomato paste

Combine meat, crumbs, parsley, chives and seasonings in a mixing bowl. Pour evaporated milk over and mix lightly with a large fork. Divide half the meat mixture among 24 greased hollows of patty pans and press into the hollows. Refrigerate together with remaining meat mixture. Prepare filling: Fry bacon and onion until onion is translucent. Remove from heat and stir in chutney and tomato paste. Allow to cool slightly. Spoon bacon mixture on top of chicken mixture in patty pan hollows. Divide remaining chicken mixture into 24 small balls and press to flatten. Place on top of filling in each hollow and press sides down firmly. Bake at 180 °C for 10-15 minutes. Allow to cool slightly in pans, remove from hollows carefully and allow to cool completely on a cooling rack.

Makes 24 chicken patties

# Jellied chicken loaf

Cut this chicken loaf into slices and use it with lettuce to make delicious sandwiches, or put it in the lunch box as a snack.

6-8 chicken pieces or 1 medium chicken
30 ml cooking oil
salt and freshly ground black pepper to taste
1 bay leaf
2 cloves stuck into an onion
250 ml dry white wine
25 ml gelatine
125 ml cooking liquid from chicken
200 ml mayonnaise
30 ml lemon juice
20 ml white vinegar
5-6 gherkins, finely chopped
3 hard-boiled eggs, crumbled
Tabasco sauce to taste
125 ml cream, stiffly whipped

Brown chicken in cooking oil. Season with salt, pepper, bay leaf and onion with cloves. Heat white wine and pour over chicken. Simmer until meat is tender and will come off the bones easily. Remove bones and cut meat very finely (reserve cooking liquid). Dissolve gelatine in 125 ml lukewarm cooking liquid. Mix dissolved gelatine, mayonnaise, lemon juice, vinegar, gherkins and eggs lightly with chicken. Season with Tabasco sauce and salt and black pepper to taste. Fold in cream. Spoon into a greased medium loaf tin, spreading evenly. Allow to set in refrigerator. Turn out and slice thinly.

Makes about 24 slices

VARIATION
* Make small individual moulds and place in lunch box, mould and all.

# Chicken loaf

1 small onion, chopped
1 clove garlic, crushed
4-5 rashers rindless bacon, shredded
15 ml cooking oil
50 ml butter
250 ml breadcrumbs
300 ml milk
4 eggs, separated
500 ml finely cut or flaked cooked chicken
salt and freshly ground black pepper to taste
5 ml dried or 15 ml chopped fresh parsley
100 g grated Cheddar cheese (250 ml)

Fry onion, garlic and bacon in heated oil in a heavy-based pan. Melt butter in a small saucepan and add breadcrumbs and milk. Bring to the boil. Remove from heat and stir in beaten egg yolks. Add chicken, seasonings, parsley and bacon mixture. Stir in cheese. Whisk egg whites until stiff and fold into chicken mixture. Turn into a greased loaf tin and bake at 180 °C for about 30 minutes or until set.

# Flavoursome meat loaf

Leave the meat loaf in the gravy until cooled.

500 g minced beef
500 g minced pork
500 ml fresh breadcrumbs
2 onions, grated
salt and freshly ground black pepper to taste
5 ml dry mustard
25 ml ordinary or tomato chutney
200 ml tomato purée
60 ml milk
2 eggs, beaten
¼ green sweet pepper, seeded and chopped
10 ml dried or 30 ml chopped fresh parsley
4 rashers rindless bacon, shredded

*Chicken loaf*

Mix all the ingredients lightly. Turn into a greased loaf tin. Bake at 160 °C for 50-60 minutes. Leave in the warming drawer for 10 minutes before turning out.

Makes 10 servings

# Rainbow silverside

Place foil-wrapped rainbow silverside in the refrigerator and use on sandwiches or as cold meat. Pep it up with a little mustard sauce or piquant chutney.

1,5 kg silverside (eye muscle)
125 g rindless bacon, cut into strips
2 cloves garlic, slivered
2 carrots, cut into strips
30 ml cooking oil
salt and freshly ground black pepper to taste

MARINADE
100 ml each meat stock, lemon juice and cooking oil
8 juniper berries (optional)
1 sprig parsley
1 bay leaf
1 onion, sliced into rings
5 black peppercorns
2 ml salt

Lard meat with bacon, garlic and carrots. Tie meat so it will retain its shape during cooking process. Mix marinade ingredients and use to marinate meat overnight. Drain and pat dry with paper towelling. Reserve marinade. Brown meat in heated oil in a heavy-based saucepan. Season. Heat reserved marinade and add to meat. Cover with lid and simmer for 2-2½ hours or until meat is tender. Allow to cool. Slice thinly.

Makes 8 servings

HINTS
* For juicier and tastier results, allow the meat to cool in the liquid in which it was cooked.
* The meat is done when a fibre can be pulled off easily.

# Takeaway neck of lamb

To save yourself trouble, ask the butcher to bone the neck of lamb. If you bake the meat in a cooking bag you will have the minimum washing up afterwards.

    25 ml cooking oil
    75 ml dry white wine
    1 stalk celery, chopped
    2 cloves garlic, crushed
    1 carrot, grated
    2 ml dried or 5 ml chopped fresh thyme
    5 ml ground coriander
    2 boned necks of lamb, about 1,5 kg
    25 ml cake flour
    salt and freshly ground black pepper to taste

Mix cooking oil, wine, celery, garlic, carrot, thyme and coriander. Rub this mixture over meat. Place meat in an airtight container and refrigerate for 4-6 hours (reserve marinade). Place flour, salt and pepper in a cooking bag and shake well. Place meat and leftover marinade in cooking bag and shake to coat meat. Loosely tie bag and place in an oven dish. Pierce the bag several times to allow steam to escape. Bake at 160 °C for 1½ hours, or 40-50 minutes per 500 g meat plus an additional 40 minutes. Remove from oven and allow to cool. Slice thinly and use for takeaway meals.

Makes 8 servings

HINT
* To pack the meat for a picnic: Place the sliced meat on one side of a large sheet of aluminium foil. On the other side, arrange lettuce leaves, hard-boiled eggs, gherkins and cherry tomatoes. Fold the foil in such a way that the meat and salad remain separate. Pack in a container with a tight-fitting lid and in a cool bag. When the foil is unfolded the guests can help themselves to meat and salad. Buttered whole-wheat bread is the ideal accompaniment.

# Curried brawn

Brawn is not merely a delicacy of bygone days, when it was prepared the day after animals had been slaughtered. It is a winner on whole-wheat bread and can be served with cold meat or even in salads.

    1 cowheel, cleaned
    1 kg beef shin
    2 cloves
    1 bay leaf
    5 peppercorns
    500 ml strained cooking liquid from beef
    2 onions, chopped
    20 ml cooking oil
    30 ml mild curry powder
    15 ml turmeric
    15 ml salt
    5 ml grated lemon rind
    50 ml apricot jam
    pinch coriander
    200 ml vinegar

Cover cowheel and beef shin with cold water. Add spices and simmer for about 3½ hours or until meat is tender. Strain cooking liquid and reserve 500 ml. Fry onions in heated oil until translucent. Add curry powder and turmeric and stir-fry for a few minutes. Add remaining ingredients along with the 500 ml cooking liquid. (Use less cooking liquid if you prefer a meatier brawn.) Bring to the boil and simmer for a few minutes. Remove bones and flake, mince or cut meat into small pieces. Add meat to curry mixture and simmer for a further 30 minutes, stirring occasionally. Pour mixture into moulds, rinsed out with cold water or sprayed with nonstick cooking spray beforehand, and allow to set.

HINTS
* Use 2 pork shanks from which the glands have been removed, and 500 g lean pork thick rib.
* Brawn can be allowed to set in empty butter tubs, and may even be frozen for short periods.

# Biltong sticks

Most South Africans still regard this salted and dried beef as the supreme delicacy. It is not only a delicious snack for the lunch box, but may also be used in sandwiches, salads, muffins or quiches.

25 kg silverside, topside or thick flank
500 g coarse salt (500 ml)
180 g brown sugar (225 ml)
20 g bicarbonate of soda (25 ml)
15 ml freshly ground black pepper
120 g scorched ground coriander*
grape vinegar

Remove as much connective tissue as possible and cut meat along the grain into strips 15-20 cm thick. Mix salt, sugar, bicarbonate of soda, pepper and coriander. Layer meat in a suitable container and sprinkle each layer with the salt mixture. Sprinkle a little vinegar over each layer and leave in a cool place for 4-6 hours. Dip meat in hot vinegar water** to remove surface salt. Hang meat to dry on wire hooks, plastic hooks or loops of string in a cool, airy place. Meat strips should not come into contact with one another, otherwise they will become mouldy. Store in a cool, dry place, or wrap in clingwrap or thick plastic, squeeze out all the air and freeze indefinitely.

Makes 12 kg biltong sticks

* Place the whole coriander in a dry frying pan, heat and stir continuously until it turns light brown. Crush in a food processor or with a pestle and mortar, or place between two layers of cloth and crush with a rolling pin. Sieve to remove husks. 15 ml whole coriander yields 5 ml ground coriander.
** Hot vinegar water is made by mixing 350 ml vinegar and 5 litres boiling water.

## How to make biltong

* Select the time of year for making biltong just as carefully as you would the meat. The best time is late autumn or winter when conditions are cold and dry. In wetter regions it is advisable to dry the meat in a biltong drier.
* Use a large, sharp knife for making neat incisions in the meat – loose bits of meat may cause mould.
* Why are bicarbonate of soda and sugar used? Bicarbonate of soda prevents mould, and sugar is added to counteract the hardening effect of the salt, thus ensuring a "softer" biltong. Since the quantity is very small it will not sweeten the biltong.
* Salt the meat in plastic, stainless steel, enamel or unchipped earthenware containers. Metal containers are unsuitable.
* Biltong may be hung indoors, provided there is a draught – an electric fan will create a good air flow.
* For ordinary biltong the meat is cut into strips 25-50 cm thick. The quantity of coarse salt is doubled and the meat is left overnight instead of for 4-6 hours.
* Optional ingredients that may be added:
  - Saltpetre: 20 g (15 ml) for 25 kg meat to give the distinctive red colour.
  - Replace the coriander with one of the following:
    Aniseed  100 g (350 ml)
    Allspice  5 ml
    Garlic salt  15 ml
    Peri-peri  10 ml
  - Replace ½ the vinegar with red wine or Worcester sauce.
* About 50-60% of the meat mass is lost in the drying process. This means that the biltong mass will only be about 40% of the original.

# Sweet treats

## Quick buttermilk rusks

Keep these foolproof rusks in an airtight jar at the office and enjoy them with your afternoon coffee.

    3 x 500 g packets self-raising flour
    5 ml each salt and cream of tartar
    300 g sugar (375 ml)
    500 g butter or margarine
    500 ml buttermilk

Sift self-raising flour, salt and cream of tartar together, then add sugar. Melt butter and add to flour mixture along with buttermilk. Mix to a dough. Shape balls and place in a greased oven pan. Bake at 180 °C for 1 hour or until a testing skewer comes out clean. Turn onto a cooling rack to cool slightly. Break open while still warm and divide into rusks. Dry out.

Makes 40 rusks depending on size

---

VARIATION
* Replace half the buttermilk with cream for a richer flavour.

---

HINTS
* Rinse out the buttermilk container with a little milk and add liquid to rusk mixture.
* Cover the rusks with aluminium foil if they brown too quickly.
* Butter imparts a better flavour, but margarine is recommended if rusks are to be stored for a long time.
* Use two forks to halve the baked balls.

*Quick buttermilk rusks and Diana's high-fibre rusks*

## Diana's high-fibre rusks

This is a sure-fire winner: ideal for breakfast, elevenses or to snack on whenever you feel peckish.

    500 g butter
    500 ml buttermilk
    300 g brown sugar (375 ml)
    280 g self-raising flour (500 ml)
    15 ml baking powder
    5 ml salt
    750 g Nutty Wheat (5 x 250 ml)
    250 ml digestive bran
    50 g All-Bran (250 ml)

Melt butter together with buttermilk and sugar. Cool slightly. Sift together self-raising flour, baking powder and salt. Add Nutty Wheat, bran and All-Bran. Stir in butter mixture and mix to a dough. Turn dough into a greased oven pan and spread evenly. Bake at 180 °C for 50-60 minutes or until a testing skewer comes out clean. Turn out onto a cooling rack to cool slightly. Break off rusks while still warm, then cool completely. Dry out.

Makes 40 rusks depending on size

---

VARIATION
* Some people prefer to make buns: Use 2 x 250 ml digestive bran, 500 g brown sugar (625 ml) and 1,5 kg Nutty Wheat (10 x 250 ml). The rest of the ingredients remain the same.

---

# Chocolate chip rusks

Children will love these rusks and polish them off in no time. They will also make teatime at the office something to look forward to.

    500 g butter or margarine
    600 ml milk
    300 g sugar (375 ml)
    1,2 kg self-raising flour (8 x 250 ml + 150 ml)
    5 ml salt
    150 g chocolate chips (250 ml)

Melt butter together with milk and sugar. Cool slightly. Sift flour and salt together. Add chocolate chips. Stir in butter mixture and mix to a dough. Turn dough into a greased oven pan and spread evenly. Bake at 180 ˚C for 45 minutes or until a testing skewer comes out clean. Turn out onto a cooling rack to cool slightly, break into rusks while still warm and cool completely. Dry out.

Makes 40 rusks depending on size

HINT
* Using a knife dipped in water, mark the dough before baking it. This will make it easier to break off rusks afterwards.

---

## How to dry out rusks

Place the rusks on a wire rack on an ungreased baking tray and dry out overnight in the warming drawer. In the oven itself rusks are dried out at the lowest temperature (about 50 ˚C) until completely dry. Shorten the drying-out process by simply placing the rusks on the oven rack, with the bottom of the oven covered with aluminium foil. Use a wooden spoon to keep the oven door slightly ajar to allow moisture to escape. Turn the rusks over to dry out the other side as well. Cool completely and store in airtight containers.

---

# All-Bran rusks with sunflower seeds

Offer some of these All-Bran rusks to your colleagues during the coffee break, and they will beg you for the recipe!

    500 g butter
    500 ml buttermilk
    15 ml vanilla essence
    840 g self-raising flour (6 x 250 ml)
    5 ml salt
    300 g sugar (375 ml)
    150 g All-Bran, slightly crushed (3 x 250 ml)
    150 g sunflower seeds (250 ml)
    75 g seedless raisins (125 ml)

Melt butter, then stir in buttermilk and vanilla essence. Sift flour and salt together. Add sugar, All-Bran, sunflower seeds and raisins, blending well. Add butter mixture to dry ingredients, mixing well until a fairly stiff dough is formed. Shape balls and place close together in 2-3 greased loaf tins. Bake at 180 ˚C for 45-60 minutes or until a testing skewer comes out clean. Turn out onto a cooling rack to cool slightly. Break open while still warm and divide into rusks. Dry out.

Makes 40-60 rusks depending on size

# Breakfast bars

Keep these rusks, that are nothing more than "dried-out muesli bars", in an airtight container at the office for those rushed mornings when you have to skip breakfast at home. Incidentally, they're just the thing for people who loathe porridge!

    1 kg self-raising flour (7 x 250 ml)
    5 ml baking powder
    3 ml salt

500 ml muesli
75 g bleached sultanas (125 ml)
75 g chopped dried apricots or pears (125 ml)
1 x 100 g packet nuts, preferably pecan nuts or walnuts
80 g coconut (250 ml)
150 g sunflower seeds (250 ml)
50 ml sesame seeds
300 g brown sugar (375 ml)
2 extra-large eggs
500 ml guava yoghurt
500 g butter, melted and froth skimmed off

Combine flour, baking powder, salt, muesli, sultanas, apricots, nuts, coconut, sunflower and sesame seeds and sugar in a large mixing bowl or dough basin. Make a hollow in mixture. Beat eggs and yoghurt together. Stir in cooled butter. Pour yoghurt mixture into centre of flour mixture and mix quickly but thoroughly with a large fork or wooden spoon. Turn into 3 greased loaf tins, spreading evenly. Bake at 180 °C for 45-60 minutes. After about 40 minutes has elapsed a piece of aluminium foil may be placed on top, shiny side up, to prevent overbrowning. Remove from oven and allow to cool in tins for 5 minutes. Turn out onto a cooling rack. Cool completely. Cut into thick slices and then into fingers. Dry out. Cool completely and store in airtight containers.

Makes 40-60 bars depending on size

VARIATION
* Replace the guava yoghurt with a yoghurt of your choice. Pineapple or banana yoghurt is particularly suitable.

# Kisses

These biscuits have few ingredients and can be made in a jiffy. Besides, you can cut down on the washing-up by lining the baking trays with baking paper or greased butter paper.

1 x 397 g tin full-cream condensed milk
320 g coconut (4 x 250 ml)
5 ml vanilla or caramel essence
pinch salt
30 glacé cherry halves

Mix all the ingredients, except glacé cherries, thoroughly. Spoon teaspoonfuls onto a greased baking tray, top with a cherry half and bake at 160 °C for 25-30 minutes. Cool on a cooling rack.

Makes 20-30 biscuits

HINT
* The biscuits are baked at a low temperature because coconut browns very quickly.

# Snow cookies

These cookies are as white as snow because of the icing sugar coating – hence the name.

250 g soft butter (250 ml)
210 g castor sugar (250 ml)
1 egg
15 ml brandy
5 ml each mixed spice and ground cinnamon
300 g cake flour (625 ml)
50 g chopped pecan nuts or walnuts (125 ml)
260 g icing sugar, sifted (500 ml)

Cream butter and castor sugar until light and creamy. Add egg and brandy and continue beating. Sift spices and flour together. Add to butter mixture along with nuts. Mix to a soft dough. Roll into walnut-sized balls between the palms of your hands and place, slightly apart, on greased baking trays. Bake at 190 °C for 7-12 minutes or until light golden. Carefully coat hot cookies with icing sugar and place on waxed paper to cool. Coat with icing sugar once more.

Makes about 5 dozen cookies

# Debra's health triangles

Oats cookies packed with breakfast cereals! If you prefer crisp cookies, cool them on a cooling rack; otherwise, leave them in the baking tray for a deliciously soft texture.

250 g butter
400 g brown sugar (500 ml)
2 eggs, beaten
280 g Nutty Wheat or brown-bread flour (500 ml)
3 ml salt
160 g oats (500 ml)
250 ml Hi-Fibre Bran (not All-Bran flakes)
250 ml ProNutro
10 ml baking powder
10 ml ground cinnamon
5 ml ground ginger

Melt butter. Add sugar and eggs, mixing well. Stir in remaining ingredients and mix well. Pour mixture into a rectangular tray (about 30 cm x 40 cm), spread evenly and bake at 180 °C for 25-30 minutes or until golden brown.

Makes 80 triangles

VARIATIONS
* Cut into 40 squares instead of triangles.
* Replace the Hi-Fibre Bran and ProNutro with 250 ml Rice Krispies and 150 g peanuts (250 ml).

HINT
* The triangles may be frozen for up to 6 months.

# Ginger nuts

The cake tin will be empty in no time if you store these biscuits in it.

*Kisses (p. 115)*

250 g butter
125 ml golden syrup
½ x 25 g packet bicarbonate of soda (15 ml)
37,5 ml milk
3 eggs, beaten
½ x 25 g packet cream of tartar (15 ml)
10 ml ginger
600 g cake flour (5 x 250 ml)
500 g sugar (625 ml)

Heat butter and syrup until butter has melted. Allow to cool. Dissolve bicarbonate of soda in milk and add to syrup mixture. Add eggs and mix well. Sift together cream of tartar, ginger and flour, then add sugar. Add syrup mixture to dry ingredients and mix to a stiff dough. Allow to cool. Shape into balls and arrange, slightly apart, on greased baking trays. Bake at 180 °C for 10-15 minutes. Allow to cool slightly on tray, then place on a cooling rack to cool completely.

Makes 160 ginger nuts depending on size

HINTS
* The baking trays need not be greased repeatedly. If 2 are used, cool 1 of them in the refrigerator.
* You do not have to flatten the balls before baking.
* A medium baking tray takes about 24 balls.

## How to bake biscuits

* It is advisable to bake only one tray of biscuits at a time. Place the tray in a preheated oven on the middle or top oven rack. If you bake more than one tray of biscuits at a time, change them around halfway through the baking time. Ensure that there is sufficient space on either side of the tray to allow hot air to circulate.
* Leave sufficient space between biscuits, as most types of dough spread during the baking process.
* The longer the baking time, the harder the biscuits will be.
* Biscuits are soft when removed from the oven and harden as they cool.

# Aunt Olaf's whole-meal shortbread

Prick the shortbread before baking to allow steam to escape and to ensure a beautifully crisp texture. The caramel and chocolate topping may be omitted, if preferred.

250 g butter
130 g icing sugar (250 ml)
140 g cake flour (250 ml)
60 g cornflour (125 ml)
2 ml salt
150 g Nutty Wheat (250 ml)

TOPPING
75 g butter
50 ml golden syrup
1 x 397 g tin condensed milk
105 g castor sugar (125 ml)
150 g dark chocolate

Cream butter and icing sugar until light and fluffy. Sift dry ingredients together and add husks remaining in sieve to flour mixture. Add to butter mixture, rubbing it in until a stiff dough is formed. Press into a lightly greased rectangular pan measuring 20 cm x 24 cm. Prick with a fork and bake at 160 °C for 45 minutes. Bring ingredients for topping, except chocolate, to the boil. Boil for 5 minutes, stirring continuously, until thickened. Spread on baked shortbread, spreading evenly with a palette knife. Allow to cool. Melt chocolate in top half of a double boiler and spread over cold caramel coating. Cut into squares just before chocolate sets. Store in an airtight container.

Makes 35 squares

# Almond and caramel bars

A cake tin containing these mouthwatering titbits will be empty in no time! A cheaper option is to replace the almonds with toasted unsalted peanuts.

125 g butter or margarine
100 g sugar (125 ml)
1 egg yolk
5 ml caramel essence
180 g cake flour (315 ml)
2 ml baking powder
25 ml custard powder
pinch salt

TOPPING
80 g soft brown sugar (100 ml)
30 ml golden syrup
100 g butter or margarine
75 g almond flakes (125 ml)

Cream butter and sugar. Add egg yolk and mix until light and fluffy. Stir in essence. Add dry ingredients and mix to a stiff dough. Press mixture into a well-greased rectangular pan measuring 20 cm x 24 cm. Bake at 180 °C for 20-25 minutes or until golden brown. Prepare topping: Place brown sugar, golden syrup and butter in a saucepan. Stir over low heat until butter has melted and sugar has dissolved. Simmer over low heat for 5 minutes. Carefully stir in almonds. Remove cake from oven, spread carefully with prepared topping and return to oven for a further 5 minutes. Allow to cool in pan, then cut into bars. Store in an airtight container.

Makes about 25 bars

# Riviera biscuits

No one will be able to resist these!

180 g butter
100 g sugar (125 ml)
1 egg, beaten
5 ml caramel essence
255 g cake flour (530 ml)
10 ml baking powder

pinch salt
125 ml coconut

FILLING
60 g butter
180 g icing sugar (350 ml)
3 ml caramel essence
10 ml milk
strawberry jam

Cream butter and sugar until light and fluffy. Add egg and essence and mix well. Sift dry ingredients together and add to butter mixture along with coconut. Mix well. Scoop out teaspoonfuls and roll into balls. Place on a greased baking tray and press to flatten. Bake at 180 ˚C for 10-15 minutes. Turn out onto a cooling rack and allow to cool. Meanwhile, prepare filling: Cream butter and icing sugar until light and fluffy. Add essence and milk and mix well. Sandwich 2 biscuits together with a little filling and strawberry jam.

Makes 15-20 double biscuits depending on size

VARIATION
* Use a jam of your choice, e.g. fig or apricot jam.

# Chocolate chip cookies

Ideal for filling empty corners in a lunch box, but just as suitable for taking along on holiday.

125 g soft butter
200 g sugar (250 ml)
1 egg
2,5 ml vanilla essence
140 g self-raising flour (250 ml)
pinch salt
2,5 ml bicarbonate of soda
15 ml cocoa (optional)

75 g chopped pecan nuts (187,5 ml)
100 g oats (300 ml)
180 g chocolate chips (300 ml)

Cream butter and sugar until light and fluffy. Add egg and essence, beating well. Sift dry ingredients together and stir into butter mixture along with nuts, oats and chocolate chips. Place teaspoonfuls on a greased baking tray, leaving enough space in between for cookies to spread. Bake at 190 ˚C for 15 minutes. Leave cookies to harden on tray for 1-2 minutes, then place them on a cooling rack.

Makes 40 cookies

HINT
* Leave about 5 cm space between cookies on the baking tray. A medium-sized baking tray has room for about 15 cookies.

## How to cool and store biscuits

* To prevent overbaking, remove biscuits immediately from the baking tray with a spatula and place on a cooling rack.
* The biscuits should be cooled completely before storing them, otherwise they will soften.
* Always store biscuits in an airtight container, and keep soft and crisp biscuits apart.
* Crisp biscuits that have softened, can be crisped again: Place them in a cool oven (150 ˚C) for 5 minutes.
* Hard biscuits which have cooled completely, may be frozen in a plastic bag or container for 2-3 months. Simply leave the biscuits at room temperature to thaw.

# Miracle squares

These mocha-flavoured cake squares can be baked and then frozen. Pack a frozen square into the lunch box, and by playtime or teatime it will taste freshly baked!

2 eggs
250 g sugar (300 ml)
250 g self-raising flour (450 ml)
30 ml cocoa
pinch salt
150 ml milk
150 g butter or margarine, melted (175 ml)
5 ml caramel essence

ICING
5 ml coffee powder
100 ml boiling water
175 g icing sugar, sifted (350 ml)
90 g butter or margarine, melted (100 ml)
30 ml cocoa
5 ml caramel essence
coconut or hundreds-and-thousands for sprinkling

Beat eggs and sugar together until light in colour. Sift dry ingredients together and stir into egg mixture, alternating with milk and butter. Stir in essence. Turn batter into a black oven pan (30 cm x 40 cm) and bake at 200 °C for 15 minutes or until a testing skewer comes out clean. Meanwhile, prepare icing: Dissolve coffee powder in boiling water. Mix icing sugar, butter or margarine, cocoa, essence and coffee until smooth. Spread over warm cake. Cool cake in oven pan, then cut into 5 cm x 5 cm squares. Sprinkle with coconut or hundreds-and-thousands for decoration.

Makes 36 squares

# Banana cake

Leave room in the lunch box for a slice of this deliciously moist cake.

300 g cake flour (625 ml)
15 ml baking powder
5 ml bicarbonate of soda
3 ml salt
300 g sugar (375 ml)
175 g butter
375 ml banana pulp
3 eggs, beaten
125 ml buttermilk or sour milk
10 ml vanilla essence
50 g chopped nuts (125 ml)

FILLING AND DECORATION
125 ml cream, stiffly whipped
½ x 389 g tin caramel condensed milk

Sift dry ingredients together. Cream sugar and butter. Add banana pulp, eggs, buttermilk or sour milk and essence, beating until well blended. Add dry ingredients and nuts, mixing well. Turn into 2 greased cake tins, each 200 mm in diameter. Spread evenly and bake at 180 °C for 30 minutes. Turn out and allow to cool. Fold cream into caramel condensed milk and spread on one cake layer. Sandwich 2 layers together. Decorate with remaining caramel mixture.

HINT
✱ Six to eight ripe bananas will yield the required quantity of pulp.

*Unbaked breakfast bars (p. 122), caramel and sultana balls (p. 124) and date and raisin balls (back, p. 123)*

# Sweet-milk cheese tart

Children usually look forward to second break so that they can polish off the last piece of tart left in the lunch box.

CRUST
120 g cake flour (250 ml)
15 ml icing sugar
pinch salt
90 g butter, cubed
1 large egg yolk
15 ml iced water

FILLING
500 g sweet-milk cheese, finely grated (5 x 250 ml)
160 g sugar (200 ml)
120 g cake flour (250 ml)
1 egg, plus 6 eggs, separated
175 ml sour cream
5 ml vanilla essence
50 g castor sugar (100 ml)

Sift together dry ingredients and rub in butter. Add egg yolk and water and mix to a dough. (Add a little more water if very crumbly.) Shape into a ball, cover with clingwrap or place in a plastic bag and refrigerate for about 30 minutes. Line a greased loose-bottomed pan, 23 cm in diameter, with pastry and refrigerate until needed. Prepare filling: Mix cheese and sugar well. Sift flour over and mix in well. Beat in egg and 6 egg yolks. Add sour cream and essence and beat until mixed. Whisk egg whites until soft peaks form. Gradually add castor sugar, whisking continuously. Fold egg whites into filling and pour into lined pan. Bake at 180 ˚C for about 1 hour or until filling is firm. Switch off oven and leave tart to cool slightly in oven, with the door slightly ajar. Turn out. Slice and take along in containers into which the slices fit snugly.

Makes 1 tart

# UNBAKED TREATS

## Unbaked breakfast bars

No child is ever satisfied with just one of these scrumptious treats in his lunch box!

125 g butter or margarine
200 g brown sugar (250 ml)
1 x 397 g tin condensed milk
80 g oats (250 ml)
80 g fine coconut (250 ml)
225 g seedless raisins (375 ml)
250 ml Rice Krispies
250 ml All-Bran flakes
melted chocolate (optional)

Microwave butter, sugar and condensed milk in a 2-litre microwave dish on 100% power for 7 minutes, stirring regularly. Mix remaining ingredients, except chocolate, and make a hollow in the centre. Spoon sugar mixture into hollow. Mix well. Turn into a shallow greased container, spreading evenly. Leave for 3 hours, then cut into bars or squares to a size of your choice. Dip entire bar/square, or just half, in melted chocolate, if preferred. Place on a cooling rack until chocolate has set.

Makes 36 bars depending on size

## White squares

These biscuits are cooked on top of the stove. For safety's sake, children should use the microwave oven.

125 g margarine or butter
1 x 500 g packet icing sugar (960 ml), sifted
3 eggs, beaten
5 ml vanilla essence
1½ x 300 g packets Marie biscuits, crushed
1 x 200 g packet coconut (625 ml)

Melt margarine or butter in a saucepan. Remove from heat, then add icing sugar and beaten eggs. Return to stove and stir until egg mixture is thick and cooked. Be very careful of burning. Remove from heat and add remaining ingredients. Press into a greased pan and allow to set. Cut into squares.

Makes 30-40 squares depending on size

VARIATIONS
* Add 1 x 100 g packet glacé cherries, chopped, along with the biscuits.
* Add 250 ml chopped nuts along with the biscuits.
* For squares that are less sweet, add only a ¾ packet of icing sugar.

HINT
* Microwave the sugar and egg mixture to cook and thicken it without burning. Microwave on 70% power for 10 minutes, stirring regularly. This method is also safer for children who want to make these biscuits themselves.

# Chocolate marshmallow squares

Children will find these marshmallow squares irresistible. They will keep for 2 weeks in an airtight container, but are too delicious to last that long!

1 25 g butter
1 x 500 g packet white marshmallows (70 sweets)
5 ml vanilla essence
350 g Rice Krispies (12 x 250 ml)
2 x 200 g slabs milk chocolate

Melt butter in a saucepan. Add marshmallows, stirring until almost melted. Remove from heat and stir in essence and Rice Krispies until just well mixed. Press into a greased baking tray. Melt chocolate in top half of a double boiler and spread over mixture. Leave to set for about 1 hour. Cut into squares.

Makes about 40 squares depending on size

VARIATION
* Use pink marshmallows and add pink food colouring to the milk chocolate.

HINT
* If you leave the mixture for too long before cutting it, it may become too hard.

# Date and raisin balls

A health snack for the lunch box.

150 g seedless raisins (250 ml)
150 g stoned dates, chopped (250 ml)
250 ml peanut butter
50 ml coconut
sesame seeds or extra coconut for coating

Process all the ingredients in a food processor and roll into 20 balls. Coat in sesame seeds or coconut. Refrigerate.

Makes 20 balls

VARIATIONS
* Chocolate nut paste may be used instead of the peanut butter.
* To make this an even more wholesome snack, replace the peanut butter with tahini – a sesame paste available from health shops or the health food shelves of some supermarkets.

# Caramel and sultana balls

Once you've started, you can't stop eating these! Caramel and sultana balls are the ideal snack for the lunch box.

  1 x 389 g tin caramel condensed milk
  1 x 200 g packet Marie biscuits, crushed
  80 g coconut (250 ml)
  75 g sultanas (125 ml)
  coconut for coating

Beat caramel condensed milk to make it more spreadable. Mix with biscuits, coconut and sultanas and shape into balls. Coat in coconut.

Makes 36-50 balls depending on size

# Fudge

Meltingly delicious and a must for the lunch box!

  1 x 397 g tin condensed milk
  420 g castor sugar (500 ml)
  125 g butter or margarine
  5 ml vanilla essence

Place all the ingredients, except essence, in a large microwave glass dish. Microwave on 100% power for 2 minutes. Beat with a wooden spoon. Microwave on 100% power for a further 10 minutes, stirring every minute. Fudge is ready as soon as it starts to subside slightly. Do not allow it to boil over. Beat again. Add essence and stir once again. Pour into a greased 25 cm x 15 cm tray. Allow to cool, then cut into 2 cm squares.

Makes 4½ dozen

# Index